My Mother, My Mentor

My Mother, My Mentor

What Grown Children of Working Mothers Want You to Know

Pamela F. Lenehan

ARCHWAY
PUBLISHING

Archway Publishing books may be ordered through booksellers or by contacting:

Archway Publishing
1663 Liberty Drive
Bloomington, IN 47403
www.archwaypublishing.com
1 (888) 242-5904

Because of the dynamic nature of the Internet, any web addresses or links contained in this book may have changed since publication and may no longer be valid. The views expressed in this work are solely those of the author and do not necessarily reflect the views of the publisher, and the publisher hereby disclaims any responsibility for them.

Any people depicted in stock imagery provided by Thinkstock are models, and such images are being used for illustrative purposes only.
Certain stock imagery © Thinkstock.

ISBN: 978-1-4808-2151-4 (sc)
ISBN: 978-1-4808-2150-7 (hc)
ISBN: 978-1-4808-2152-1 (e)

Library of Congress Control Number: 2015951928

Print information available on the last page.

Archway Publishing rev. date: 10/07/2015

To Sarah and Paul
who gave me my best job ever ... mother

Acknowledgments

I would first like to thank the sixty-eight individuals who shared their stories, each of whom was interviewed separately. There were tears (the working mothers) and laughter (mothers and grown children) as they discussed the fun and challenges of family life with a working mother and as a working mother. Many said the interview generated deeper discussions between mothers, children, and siblings. Without them and their candor, this book would not have been possible. There is more detail on the families in the appendix so you can get to know them a little better.

The survey was created in collaboration with Natasha Fevre and Kaitlyn Krauskopf, two remarkable women I met through the Center for Women & Enterprise. Their insights and skill with survey tools made all of the data possible. I also thank them for their views of what is important to prospective working mothers.

To Kelly Epperson, thank you for being a tough editor. You kept me on track to keep the purpose of the book focused on what working mothers need to hear. I appreciate your counsel, edits, and encouragement.

Finally, to Anne Szostak, who had the original idea for this book, thank you for starting the conversation, your work in the early stages, and your guidance and advice along the way. We had parallel careers but did not meet until our children were grown and on their own. I wish I had known you during those early years of my career when I was raising children and working full time. We could have provided each other moral support and shared ideas. I hope this book will provide advice and encouragement for working mothers who are raising children today.

Contents

Chapter 1

How This Conversation Started

Women who entered the workforce in the 1970s and 1980s did so with high expectations. The women's movement of the 1960s and 70s had gained strength, and its charismatic leaders told women they could do anything they wanted if they got a good education and worked hard. At that same time, there was a generational divide over politics, music, and many other topics. The younger generation listened to rock 'n roll, grew their hair long, and disagreed with their parents on just about everything. As teenagers and then college students, they wanted to rebel. Society was also changing. Divorce rates, which were 26 percent in 1960, had jumped to 51 percent by 1979. (U.S. Census Bureau)

Young women compared the excitement of the feminist movement to their mother's lifestyle, and there was no contest. Young women wanted (and felt they needed) to have a career as well as a family. Their mothers were confused by their daughters' choices. Not many of these mothers could provide specific advice on how to do that since very few had "careers." If the mothers worked at all, it was a part-time job or they went to work after their children were grown. Their parents had "traditional marriages," where the mother stayed at home, and they could not imagine the challenges that awaited their daughters in managing both a career and family life.

I was one of the women who entered the workforce in 1974. Fresh out of college with a BA and MA in economics, and newly married, I moved to New York City and started work in the credit training program of The Chase Manhattan Bank. There were no role models. Women before me left when they had children and did not return. When I had my first child five years later, I did not know one other woman at the bank who was a working mother.

Even when other women started to have children and remained in the workforce, we did not talk about our home life. There were no pictures of our children in our offices. No email groups of "working moms" (no email!). No LinkedIn groups of working mothers. No Facebook friends to give us advice. We were each in our own silo, isolated, insecure, and unsupported. The "sisterhood" of the feminist movement did not extend to the office.

Years later, my friend Anne Szostak and I began talking about the critical question working mothers of our generation wanted to know. How did the children of this first wave of working women turn out? It was a question that lingered over current working mothers as well. Whenever Anne or I would meet younger working mothers, or women planning families in the future, the one piece of career advice they wanted was how to manage work and family responsibilities.

Along with advice and reassurance, we wanted to give them more than just our own experiences. We wanted information about and from the children of working mothers. We wanted to hear the children's feedback and perspective on growing up with a mother who had a career outside the home.

Looking for answers, we found very little on the subject. Books were either entirely from the perspective of the mothers or were academic studies of young children. We felt that vital information was missing. We wanted to know what the children themselves thought of their experiences and how the working mothers had fared. To answer these questions, we decided we had to research the subject and then write this book. Our generation has always thought we could do it all.

We decided to talk to other working mothers and their now-grown children, which we defined as twenty-three years or older. We believed that children of this age would have enough perspective to comment on the impact of a working mother and provide objective evidence of how they had fared.

We started with our own networks, but it was more difficult than we imagined since some women did not have children (at that time there were few medical options if pregnancy did not happen on its own) and others had had children later in life, so they were still teenagers. To get geographic diversity and the age requirement for the children, we reached out to colleagues and friends of friends. In the end, twenty-seven families were interviewed, which included sixty-eight mothers and children. We did not to talk to fathers because the focus was on working mothers and their children.

The interviews with the mothers and grown children offered stories and advice and provided the inspiration for the questions for an additional tool for the research, an independent online survey. Survey Monkey was chosen for its database of three million potential respondents who participate in return for a donation by the company to charity. Survey Monkey provided completed surveys from more than 1,000 people in order to get a large enough group at both ends of the spectrum: mothers who worked from the time their children were born and mothers who stayed home to raise their children through high school. The only screen was age of the respondents who ranged from twenty-three to forty-four years old.

Working mothers put in long hours at work and at home. They worry about the impact their careers and being away from home will have on their children. They want (and need) to know that their children will be okay and it is all worthwhile. If a working mother comes from a family where her own mother stayed at home, she may find that she questions herself even more.

This book is not intended to answer the question of whether or not a mother should work outside the home. That decision is left to each woman, and we should support each other's choices. Every mother is a working woman—some just get paid for work outside the home. This is book is not just for working mothers. Even if you are currently at home with your family, your sister, friend, daughter, or niece may be struggling with the question of whether her work impacts her children.

Note that when discussing the survey results, mothers who work outside the home are referred to as "working mothers." As mentioned earlier, it is a given that mothers who choose to stay at home work hard. It became an issue of semantics: "employed mothers" or "career mothers," etc. For simplicity and space, the survey results used the labels "mothers worked" and "mothers stayed at home" to differentiate. All mothers work. Enough said.

There is no guarantee any child will be as happy and well-adjusted as mothers would like. Every parent knows you can raise two children in exactly the same way, and they will still be different. Children have their own personalities, and there is something to be said for nature vs. nurture.

The issue for working mothers is not how their children will turn out, but whether they will turn out any differently if she works or if she stays at home. This book will provide working mothers with the confidence that their children will be fine. The statistics and stories that follow will show that the children of working mothers not only survived, but thrived.

Children will be children, and parenting has difficult moments whether both parents are employed outside the home or not. Certainly, there are challenges inherent in being a working mother, and ways to handle those challenges will be addressed throughout each chapter.

The following chapters will look at questions from the survey and delve into the stories from the mothers and now-grown children who were interviewed. These narratives illustrate what the children and mothers thought worked well and what working mothers need to pay special attention to as they raise their children.

To wrap up the book, working mothers and their grown children relate their different views of what success means to them and offer advice to working mothers on raising children while having a career. Topics for further discussion, short biographies of the families interviewed, and more detail on the demographics of the survey participants are included in the appendices.

Why the title *My Mother, My Mentor*? The children interviewed related many stories of how their mothers helped them through all stages of growing up and continue to be a source of advice about the workplace and personal relationships. It turns out the children realized their mothers also make wonderful mentors. It was best summed up by Deborah, one of the grown children interviewed:

> I have the opportunity to give advice a lot and I start out by saying, "I am the child of a working mother. I promise you now that your kids won't hate you."

I then go on to say, "There are moments that are really challenging to deal with, but longer term, you will have a vibrant relationship with your children with a knowledge base that expands far beyond the playground and classrooms. They will invite you into their professional world, where you have expertise. You are a continual resource to them. The early years of balancing work and kids are hard, but I talk to my mother about how to get a job, negotiating a raise, office politics, and career development. I wouldn't trade what I got from her for the world."

Chapter 2

Work: My Mother Taught Me My Work Ethic

Every mother desires to instill in her children a strong work ethic. There is no question "work" is important, be it doing chores or school work, but working mothers often worry that their own work schedules are adversely affecting their children. They fear that their working hard may not be viewed as a positive by their children.

Work Is Normal

What was gratifying for working mothers to realize was that their children were very accepting of their work. In fact, the children didn't even give it much thought at all, and when they were asked to think about it, the grown children were grateful for the lessons they learned from having a working mother.

The survey results show that daughters thought more about both parents working than sons did and daughters missed both parents more. However, when asked about how they felt about their mother working, only 18 percent of daughters strongly agreed with the statement "Missed her and/or was unhappy about her working" (vs. 13 percent for sons) and 20 percent of daughters strongly agreed with the statement "Didn't think about it" (vs. 34 percent for sons).

The survey and interviews showed that mothers were overly concerned about the impact their working had on

their offspring. All the anguish these mothers had about
working while their children were young was not necessary;
it was lost on their children. What mothers saw as sacrifices,
children saw as ordinary.

The interviews and the survey results revealed time and time
again that the children of working mothers did not think
their mothers' careers unusual or extraordinary. Mom went
to work every day. That was just the way it was. It was a fact,
not a cause for questioning.

When they are young, children are oblivious to many facets
of adult life. Their world is just that. They go to school, Mom
goes to work, they play with their friends, they take dance
lessons or play soccer, they do their homework; it all just
is. They don't wonder if working is a guilt-riddling, worry-
inducing decision for Mom.

In the survey, many grown children of working mothers
reported being proud of their working parents. It is interesting
that all children were more proud of their mothers working
than their father. Perhaps even at a young age, they realized
the efforts their mother was making for them. The chart
below indicates the percentages of grown children who, when
asked how they felt about their mother working, strongly
agreed with "Proud of her and/or thought she was a good
role model."

Some working mothers might be discouraged by the statistic
that only 53 percent of daughters and 43 percent of sons
strongly agreed they were proud of their working mother
at the time they were young (vs. for fathers; 34 percent of
daughters and 37 percent of sons strongly agreed they were
proud of their fathers). Remember, all children are self-
centered. Why should children be "proud" of something they

see as "normal?" Don't despair. As will become clear shortly, children gained deeper respect for their mothers as they grew up.

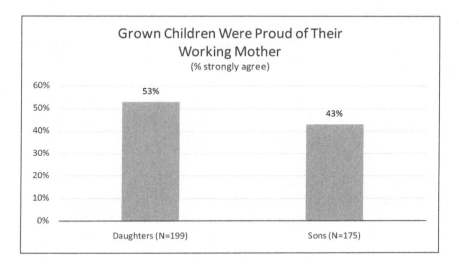

Sylvia was like many mothers who both liked working and also had to work to help support her family. Her daughter Lauren J only knows her mother as a working mother; she says, "I was fine with it. I didn't know anything different. I thought it was the norm and still do."

It is the norm. Whether by choice or by economic need, mothers work. It is not a disservice to your children to do so. In fact, your living example of taking pride in your work makes more of an impact than you realize. Not only do children understand that a working mother is normal, they also understand that hard work is rewarded and that you can follow your passions.

Marcia always had a heavy travel schedule, but her daughter Anne felt fine about her mother working. Looking back now, Anne has a better sense of the pressures her mother might have felt. Anne states it clearly: "I thought all mothers worked. This whole expectation of what a mother is supposed to be is influenced by society. A child accepts reality as it is."

Society does, even in this century, put pressure on mothers and their choice to work. A Pew Research study in April 2014 showed that 60 percent of Americans thought children were better off when one parent stayed home. Only 35 percent stated that they felt the children were fine when both parents worked. ("Breadwinner Moms," p. 10)

It's no wonder mothers today still feel angst. Occasionally, working mothers face this prejudice in the workplace. Only a few years ago, when a colleague I will call Irene mentioned it was her daughter's birthday, a well-intentioned man said, "Irene! You must feel terrible about missing your daughter's birthday!" Irene replied politely, "My children know all birthdays happen on Saturdays and Sundays." Of course weekends are when children have birthday parties, but it can be hard to not feel the sting when someone makes a thoughtless remark or you feel your mothering skills are being attacked.

Mothers still get messages from the media (and sometimes colleagues) that they are not doing right by their children if they work. The interviews and survey results showed that children were no worse off when their mother worked. In many cases, the appreciation and respect deepened when the child got older and could understand more of what their mother really did.

Children Get a Strong Work Ethic from Working Mothers

The topic of work ethic was asked in the survey in the context of helping children look for employment, but the grown children interviewed made it clear that their mother's good example of working hard was a pervasive influence throughout their childhood. Many parents instilled a strong work ethic in their children, but working mothers stood out.

Kevin states, "I got my strong work ethic from my mother. I have respect for her sacrifices and what she had to give up. To me, her working was a completely positive thing. The trade-off on both sides was totally worth it."

Lauren H says, "My mom always worked and that's just how things were. She wore two hats and she was really good at it. She has a 'can-do' attitude and she wants us to live to our highest potential. Even now she inspires me more than ever. She has done everything she set out to do. She constantly encouraged us and set a good example."

David B and his brother Jeffrey were raised primarily by their mother Toni. David remembers his mother doing everything at home, working full time at a law firm, doing pro-bono legal work, and being a community leader. "My mother never preached to us, but she taught us the importance of having a strong work ethic by demonstrating it every day."

Working mothers had more of an impact on their children than the fathers did, and daughters were especially influenced by a working mother. The chart below indicates answers under a category "Have you found your mother helpful with job searches or your work experience at any point in your career?" and the specific selection was for "Instilled a strong work ethic." The percentages were for "very helpful."

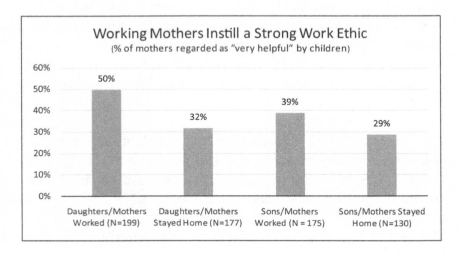

In talking about her mother Kathleen, Alix says, "Her biggest influence has been on my work ethic. I believe I can do whatever I put my heart into. She has become my biggest and greatest supporter. I see her work so hard and see the time and effort she puts into her job and her family. I want to emulate her. She worked her way up from a waitress to an executive position. If she can do it, I can do it."

Drew remembers of his mother Lisa C, "She taught me that working hard is very much a part of life. I have seen how hard she worked, including nights and weekends. Hard work is positive and is not something to resent, but it leads to a lot of success. I was always very impressed with Mom and her career path."

Rick remembers his mother Myra being very specific about what her children could do with their lives. "There were some core values she instilled in my sisters and me: hard work and discipline. You make your own success, no one will do it for you. It's up to you and you alone to define success and your own life."

Myra's daughter Jean remembers waitressing and complaining to her mother about how little money she was making. Her mother replied that Jean could change that if she wanted. Jean states, "My mom thinks you can do whatever you want to do. She pounded into our heads that we create what happens to us."

Holly, another daughter of Myra, echoed her siblings' sentiments about their mother. "Mom would say, 'Never take no for an answer. There is a limitless resource inside of yourself and your only limits are in your head.' She demonstrated that in countless ways."

Justin was asked what his mother Susan C taught him to be successful in life and he said, "Hard work. She is constantly working. She sits in front of a computer, and in my job, I use my body physically, but she taught me if you want something you have to work hard."

Maggie feels she learned a lot by watching her mother, Susan D. "There was a time period of about six months when my mother was unhappy at work and would come home and let off steam and complain about work. But hearing her complain and watching her still go to work was a great example for me. Her work ethic naturally rubbed off on me."

Working Mothers Broke Down Gender Stereotypes

With both parents working, many fathers pitched in with the work at home. The parent who arrived home the earliest was often the cook, and in many cases it was the father. What is interesting is the children did not think it was unusual. Having two working parents also changed the way these adult children now feel about their own partners, career, and home life balance.

Joanne worked long hours and had a long commute. Her husband finished work by 3:00 p.m., so he usually prepared dinner for their two daughters. Joanne's daughter Megan said, "I remember at school making Christmas gifts for our parents. The teacher had us make a potholder for our mother and a key chain for our father. When I took them home I reversed them because my father always cooked dinner and he was the one who needed the potholder. I don't think I ever told the teacher, but it made more sense for our family to do it that way."

Susan M's husband also had more predictable hours than she did. Daughter Nicole remembers, "My dad was Mr. Mom. He came home from work and cooked dinner. Two days a week he went to the gym so those nights we would microwave leftovers. Saturday night we all went out. Dad also shopped and did laundry."

Monique remembers things the same as her sister Nicole, "Dad was home at 5:30 p.m. every day, cooked, played basketball with us, and attended every extracurricular event. Weekends he was up first and I'd watch a few cartoons and by 9:30 a.m. on Saturday, Dad and I were out running errands."

Every family creates their own normal. Having a mother who worked was normal, and having a father who cooked and did "domestic" tasks was also viewed as normal. Normal is in the eye of the beholder. Children also just assumed the job their mother had was traditional for that gender. Laura H remembers that when her sons were young, one asked, "Can boys be lawyers too?"

Being a working mother and creating a home life where the children are taken care of is all that matters. Dividing the task list is an individual and personal matter. Children with working parents are more apt to be understanding of what it takes and are able to navigate these challenges in their own adult life.

Peter D believes having a working mother has changed the way he thinks about marriage. "Sons with mothers like mine might look at their wives differently. We were always told you can divide things evenly and you can both work. When I got married, I realized the reality. At some point, someone's career takes off. It doesn't have to be the man's responsibility to be the breadwinner all the time. You must allow the woman to be the person who steps into that role. I have an extremely intelligent wife, and I need to give her the space to run."

Children Don't Want Their Mothers to Feel Guilty

Yet the issue of guilt persists. Published in 1999, the "Ask the Children" study by Ellen Galinsky, president of The Families and Work Institute, reflected the ambivalence adults feel about working when it is not an economic necessity.

The study asked employed parents how they felt about mothers working who could afford to stay home. The result was: "Overall 47.5 percent agree that mothers who really don't need to earn money shouldn't work compared to fully 97 percent who agreed 'it is okay for mothers to work if they really need the money.'" (p. 9) It is no wonder that working mothers feel conflicted, but the children surveyed for this book who had two working parents do not agree with those survey results.

If you work by choice, by need, or a combination of factors, the choice is yours, and your children accept it. For most working parents, it is an economic decision.

I was a single parent for over a decade. My first husband left when my children were three and seven years old, paid no alimony, and only paid child support for a few years. I was very glad to have a good job and never felt guilty about bringing home a paycheck my family needed. I have often wondered if it was easier for me to be a working mother than for some of my married friends because I knew I had no choice but to work.

The best validation of my working came when my daughter Sarah was a senior in college and attended a career information session for a large investment bank. During the Q&A time, the only senior woman from the bank was asked, "Do you have children?" She replied yes and the questions continued. "How much do you travel?" "Who watches your children while you are away?" It was an indication that college women were thinking ahead to the issues they might face in the future.

My daughter noticed that the woman got a bit emotional while answering the questions, and when the crowd thinned out at the end of the presentation, Sarah went up to the woman to speak with her. "I just want you to know that my mother was a partner at an investment banking firm for years, and my brother and I turned out just fine." The woman said gratefully, "Thank you. I needed to hear that right now."

If the guilt rises up, know that your children do not want you to feel guilty. You also do not have to defend your reason to work, no matter what that is. You do not have to apologize.

In the interviews, children did not like it when the mother became defensive about working.

A grown child interviewed said, "I wish Mom was less defensive about being a working mother. She was good at what she did and I only knew her as a working mom, but she had a real chip on her shoulder about working. When we got into an argument she'd fall back to, 'I'm just the worst mother.' She would take the argument and turn it around and make it all about her. I wish she had less guilt. I wish she had stopped apologizing."

It is a good lesson. If you feel guilty about working, turn to other mothers or friends to voice your concerns. Children, especially adolescents, will not be very sympathetic. Also, remember all mothers have arguments, disagreements, and frustrations with their children. The fact that you are a working mother does not make parenting any harder, and being a stay-at-home mother does not make parenting any easier. Parenting is challenging. Be reassured that children with working mothers turn out just as well as those in households where the mother stays home.

As They Mature, Children Appreciate Their Mothers More

As children got older, they became proud of their working mothers, even if they did not always articulate it as kids. When the children grew up and became adults themselves, they realized how difficult it could be to manage a job and a family.

Caitlyn developed a deeper understanding of why her mother worked and what it entailed. She said, "My perspective has changed throughout my life. I first thought my mom working was normal. Then I went through a phase in middle school where I was angry and rebelled, which I call my 'angry years.' Then I became proud of her. Now I am building a relationship with her in a different way. In high school, I didn't realize how much it impacted me. I was always extremely impressed by my parents and proud of them. When I was in college and later, I realized how much she went through and how difficult it must have been for her."

Sarah D spoke for many children when she said, "Looking back now, I don't know how she did it. I always felt she was present."

Deborah, herself now a working mother of two young daughters, said, "In elementary school when I was a kid, I was fairly resentful about not having my mother pick me up from school and play with me. My mom wasn't the typical mother in her spare time—she didn't bake cookies, for example. But by high school I became proud of her and her success."

Somehow Deborah equated being a working mother with not being domestic. If her mother Judy had stayed home, she might not have placed any more importance on baking. Enjoyment of "domestic" activities depends on the woman, not with working outside of the home. As we will discuss later, cooking and baking is a great bonding time for many families with working mothers.

My own mother spent many of her adult years at home, but she was a terrible cook and her idea of creating Halloween costumes included liberal use of Scotch tape and a stapler. Some mothers simply spend their time doing things that are more meaningful to them than on the tasks traditionally expected of them.

Anne grew up with a working mother. When she was young, she told her mother at one point that she wanted to be a stay-at-home mother when she grew up. Her mother Marcia did not take this as a criticism of her own choice.

Anne remembers it this way. "I wanted to be a lot of things when I was young. When we were learning about the space program in school, I wanted to be an astronaut and wrote to NASA and got a lot of cool pictures. Then I wanted to be a vet because I liked dogs. Then I realized some people stayed home and I thought that would be fun, so I wanted to be a stay-at-home mom. Then when my mother was redecorating, I wanted to be an interior decorator. Then I wanted to be an engineer and started taking a lot of math and science courses." It is nice to know that for some children the job of being a mother is equivalent to being an astronaut!

The heart of the matter is not that Mom works. It simply boils down to the fact that children do not like being different from other children when they are young. If they live in a neighborhood where a lot of the mothers stay at home, the child might question why their mother works when other mothers do not. What working mothers sometimes forget is the opposite is also true.

My daughter told me a story about her friend, Sandy, who was starting a business and working from home. Sandy's daughter was in a preschool where a lot of nannies came to pick up the children. Sandy, who did not have a nanny, picked up her own daughter who complained, "Why can't I have a nanny pick me up like my friends do?" It is not about having a working mother. It is about being the same as the other kids.

Chapter 3

Childcare: My Mother Taught Me Many People Love and Care for Me

As working mothers know, childcare is a constant challenge. They frequently worry about it when their children are young. Parents have to go to work even when schools have snow days and teacher conferences. The matter of childcare can be all-consuming for a working mother, especially when children are young. Ask any new mother and she will tell you—deciding upon childcare can be the most grueling decision; and making it work throughout the child raising years can seem like such a challenge.

Interestingly, many mothers interviewed thought everyone else's childcare solutions must be better than their own. Parents who used daycare centers envied families with a nanny or babysitter in the house. Parents with in-home care were jealous of the built-in backup that a childcare center provided since they had all experienced a childcare crisis when the babysitter had her own life crisis. No matter how good the arrangements may seem, problems can arise. However, believe it or not, the perceived challenge of childcare does not have lasting effect.

Challenges of Childcare Fade Quickly

Looking back, the parents and children interviewed had very little to say about childcare. As long as the childcare was high quality, it all worked. What was once a working mother's primary focus had been relegated to the "necessary but not important" category. The interviews and the survey revealed the same response: Childcare was not a permanent issue.

In the survey, respondents were allowed to check more than one option when listing their childcare during preschool, elementary, middle, and high school years. The results indicated that top three providers of childcare for children of working mothers in the early years were family members, childcare centers, and the mothers themselves.

It is interesting that the children remember their mother working full time and yet taking care of them as well. As discussed below, it is possible the parents used a split shift or tag team system, or other creative ways to work and take care of their children. It is evident that working mothers did a very good job making their children feel loved and cared for.

Using family members as childcare in elementary school was mentioned by 43 percent of the grown children of working mothers in the survey, yet a 2012 AARP survey said that only 16 percent of grandparents today provide childcare while parents are at work. ("New AARP Study")

The mothers interviewed used all different types of childcare: daycare, full-time nanny, part-time outside care, and family. The type of childcare used depended on the parents' schedule and the cost and availability of the options.

A working mother has to find the right childcare option that suits her, and this can change as children grow. Just as children don't think much about their mother working, they don't know any different when it comes to childcare. It just is. Each family decides what is right for them. There are many benefits to a child experiencing good childcare. What matters is that the child feels secure and cared for.

All Are Excellent Options

• Childcare Centers

Daycare was a common option for the families interviewed since many daycare centers have operating hours long enough to cover the full work day plus commute. For many working mothers, this was the best choice.

Working mother Sylvia had access to a wonderful town-owned day care center that had programs from pre-school through sixth grade so she could have both of her children in the same place. The center was open when school was closed. The employees worked for the town and had good pay and benefits, so there was a lot of longevity. The most "junior" member Sylvia remembers meeting at the daycare center had been there for eight years.

There are many wonderful daycare centers and options that have longstanding, trusted employees along with hours that accommodate parents' schedules. Working mothers can research their own town, get referrals, and do some shopping around to find a daycare center that meets their needs. Many offer preschool and some offer kindergarten as well.

• Staggering Work Times

Some families relied on a "tag team" approach by staggering the working hours of the parents. For those who do not want to use daycare, or don't have the budget to do so, and do not have family in town, this arrangement may be an option.

Lisa B and her husband decided to take on the childcare arrangement between the two of them when their two children were young. Lisa was a consultant and her husband was a physician who worked in an emergency room in twelve-hour shifts three days a week. They used their flexible schedules to their advantage.

Lisa remembers, "We decided we did not want a full-time or live-in nanny. We had no family who could help. My husband worked his shifts and I did consulting that allowed for work at home. One parent was at home as much as possible. We only had babysitters eight to ten hours a week."

Lisa states it was not always easy, especially during the long winter months when she felt trapped inside by the weather. "I hated those sleety, awful days when you couldn't go outside. There is only so much finger painting you can do, and you can't have the TV on all day long. My husband was working all weekend in the ER and we were new in town, so I did not have a community. Grocery shopping became the highlight of my day."

Still, Lisa does not regret the choices they made as a couple. "We made a decision how we would structure that part of our lives. We would stay engaged and progress in our careers, but we wanted flexibility." She went on to say, "We made a conscious decision to handle it this way. My husband would dash in and I'd dash out. We did not realize our full earnings potential for that decade, but it was our choice."

This arrangement may have slowed their careers in the short term, but it was a decision they made as a couple. "The point is we had very deliberate conversations about what was important to us. It was a *we*, not just what *I* was going to do." After ten years of this arrangement, Lisa went into a corporate job with more structured hours, and by then her children were in school and she felt more comfortable leaving them.

- Home Daycare

Home daycare is another alternative. It worked beautifully for Joanie and her three girls, who used a trusted and beloved daycare provider, Judy. Joanie says, "I never worried a single minute the kids were with Judy. To this day she is a presence in our lives. She trained them all. She gave them good manners. She taught them to cross the street. They were there fifty hours a week." Her daughter Caitlyn remembers, "I loved Judy's. It was such fun. We'd go on a parade for Halloween."

- Nannies

Nannies were often the childcare of choice for parents who traveled or had long commutes because they could not predict their hours. Many children have wonderful memories of their nannies.

Nick said, "We always had a babysitter who was a cross between an older sibling and a parent. We had one, Rick, who was from Columbia, and I got a lot of companionship and guidance from him. He filled that gap where I could ask him questions during the week when my parents were at work or traveling." Rick became like a member of the family. Nick stated, "We stayed in touch, and I am now the godfather to his daughter."

Sarah D said, "We always had an *au pair*, and they were wonderful. They were like older sisters who always wanted to do things with us. They would pick us up at the bus stop and made sure we got all of our homework done before we were allowed to do anything else."

The nannies who were part of the children's lives for years were beloved and were viewed as a kind of substitute for the parents when they were not there. Also, during adolescence when children and parents are not always on the best of terms, having a buffer was seen as a good thing. Peter D said, "I was very close to the nannies I grew up with. Brenda filled a tremendous role in my life. When I was a teenager, I was a little brash, and she embodied 'real.' She acted *in loco parentis*, and I loved her. We would talk about conflicts I had at school or whether I was interested in a girl. She would tell me what she thought and not beat around the bush. It was good to have her there."

Peter's sister Maggie had a similar description of Brenda. "My relationship with my nanny Brenda was like another mom. She didn't go to college. She is very different from my mom and helped me with my friend problems. Brenda would say very straightforward things like 'Don't cry over spilt milk' or 'You don't need them. They are not your friends.' She is still very close to my family."

• Babysitters

When Lisa, discussed in the tag team option above, went back to work full time, the family hired a woman in her sixties, Mrs. W, to help with after school care. Mrs. W, who was an assistant at a local church, brought arts and craft materials to their home. Daughter Laura has great memories of creating art projects with Mrs. W and being taught manners and moral lessons.

Adults other than parents can have a significant impact on the children's lives, and this can be wonderful. If it takes a village to raise a child, a loving village is what it takes. Among the interviewees, not many had family members available who could provide childcare. Various options were used and all were happy with the caring, loving environment for their children.

Every family determines what is right for them. Daycare, using family members, doing a tag team approach, a home day care, in-home, and live-in help—there is no right or wrong, only what is right for the family.

Need for Childcare Decreases as Children Grow

In middle and high school, an increasing percentage of the children of working mothers surveyed listed "took care of self" as their form of childcare. By middle school, 47 percent of these children said they took care of themselves, and by high school the number rose to 63 percent.

The percentage of children of stay-at-home mothers who replied that they took care of themselves was 17 percent in middle school and 35 percent in high school. This number of children of stay-at-home mothers who said they watched out for themselves is interesting. Working mothers need to remember that even if other mothers are not working for pay, they are not necessarily sitting at home waiting for their children to return from school. They may be involved in the community, have elder care duties, or have their own activities. Not working does not equate to being with the children every minute.

Just because the children of working mothers were not in childcare did not mean they were going home to an empty house. As we will see later, the children of mothers who worked were spending more time in sports and other activities than children whose mothers were at home.

Caroline D talked about the time after school when her mother was still at work. "Mom was less involved, and since my sister and I were not micromanaged, we became more independent. We had our own schedule and managed our afternoons. Sure, we had more opportunity to screw up, but we didn't."

Working mothers take advantage of after-school programs and sports to "watch" children, but the children themselves think they are in charge. It's a good solution for everyone.

Childcare Arrangements Adapt to Mothers' Needs Too

Childcare needs change over time, and working mothers understand there is no way to "solve" the problem just once. When I lived in the city and had a short commute, we had a babysitter come to the house. I left early in the morning while my husband waited for the babysitter to arrive, and I was home by her departure time. When we moved to the suburbs and had a longer, less certain commute, we had a five-day-a-week live-in nanny, which provided us more flexibility.

During the early years, I preferred older women who were very maternal. As my children grew (and became more challenging to authority figures), I had a series of graduate students who lived in full time but were only "on duty" for the before and after school hours during the school week. These younger women were wonderful role models and did an excellent job of not taking the demands of adolescents very seriously. They taught my children everything from how to care for our first dog to making sushi. Once I was a single parent, these women helped with running errands as well as providing childcare. When my youngest got his driver's license and we no longer needed childcare, I was very sad. I thought every working mother needed someone to help run the household.

When making your decision, get the best childcare you can afford, especially when your children are young. Be flexible, and do what is right for the family, not just the children. Parents are more set in their ways than children, so find a solution that makes you feel comfortable.

Don't worry that you are not at home with your children all the time. Children benefit from different people and environments. Knowing that whatever option you choose is the right one will take some of the angst off a working mother's plate. Knowing that the grown children look back at their caretakers with affection and fondness can also ease a mother's worry. The understanding that others love them and can take care of them will serve your children well.

Chapter 4

School Years: My Mother Taught Me School Is Important

The survey and interviews confirmed what everyone knows, each level of schooling—elementary, middle, and high school—has its own challenges for children. Working mothers worry about the amount of time they are able to spend with their children and how involved they can be at school. All mothers, whether working or not, need to remain engaged and monitor their children's progress in school.

The grown children surveyed reported that as they got older their grades declined. This was across the board for children of working mothers and stay-at-home mothers. The numbers were from the general question, "Please evaluate your general school experience at each level through high school," and the option chosen was "Generally good grades."

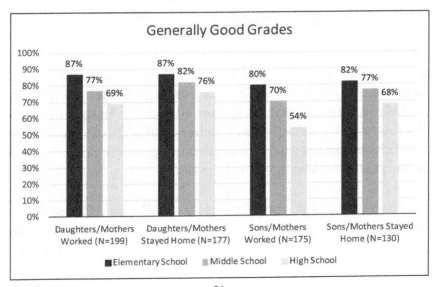

Daughters reported doing better than sons on grades for all school levels. Daughters of both working and stay-at-home mothers did well in elementary school, with 87 percent reporting good grades. In middle school, fewer daughters of working mothers reported good grades (77 percent), a level not reached by the daughters of stay-at-home mothers until high school.

Sons reported good grades at about the same level in elementary school (80 percent for sons of working mothers vs. 82 percent for sons whose mothers stayed home), then following a pattern similar to their sisters, sons of working mothers reporting good grades declined to 70 percent in middle school (vs. 77 percent for sons of stay-at-home mothers).

I was surprised when I saw these results, but apparently it is widely known within the academic community that grades in core subjects like language arts and math decline when children transition from elementary school to middle school, and then drop again when they move into high school.

In spring 2012, *Education Next* reported on two major studies in New York and Florida. ("Middle School Plunge") The studies showed a decline in grades from elementary to middle school. Why the drop? Even the experts do not know exactly why this happens. The supposition is that middle school is not as conducive a place to learn as elementary school. As a parent I can understand this. Children go from having most of their learning in one classroom to moving classrooms and dealing with many different teachers. All of this is happening at a time when they are going through puberty and trying to understand the changes in their bodies.

Another study by The University of Chicago Consortium on Chicago Schools Research, reported in a research brief in April 2014 ("Free to Fail"), found a decline in grades by

89 percent of the students when they moved from middle school to high school. The data showed that students missed many more classes and spent much less time on home work in high school than in middle school. The conclusion was that since there is much less adult monitoring in high school and teachers expected students to take charge of their own learning, many students failed to step up to the responsibility.

Why the differences between children of working mothers and mothers who stayed at home seen in the survey for this book? It could be the mothers who stayed at home had more time to keep their children focused on academics. It may also be that since the children of working mothers reported higher involvement in sports and other activities at all school levels than children of stay-at-home mothers (which we will see later), they spent less time on schoolwork. The working mothers may have decided that keeping their children engaged in a variety of activities was better for them than just being focused on academics.

I wish I had known more about school transitions when my children were young, but I knew that whenever they changed schools it was difficult. My son Paul was not very forthcoming about what went on during the school day (everything was "fine,") but my daughter Sarah's description of middle school made it sound chaotic when compared to elementary school. We lived in a very good public school district, but even at our middle school there were fights in the classroom and bullying.

Very early in their school careers my children had their own opinions about what was important or not and I was okay with that, to a point. My son only worked hard in subjects that interested him—until high school when his sister reminded him grades actually did count if he wanted to go to college.

My daughter was more competitive about grades, but even she had a slump in middle school. By college, both of my children were in completely in charge of their own education and ended up going on to get MBAs. They were the ones who decided how hard they would work; I could not do the schoolwork for them. All a mother can do is set an example and provide a good environment for children to be successful.

The decline in reported grades did not bar entry into college. The survey showed the final education level of the children was impacted primarily by the education level of the mother, not whether the mother worked or not. The answers below were to the question, "What is your highest level of education?" The percentages combine the choices of bachelor's degrees and advanced degrees (Master's, MBA, MD, JD, PhD).

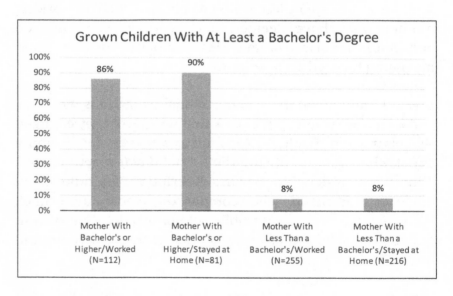

It turned out the "final report card" was equal. A child's grades did not affect the ending level of academic achievement. It may be helpful for working mothers to remind themselves of this.

Mothers Need to Stay Involved

Working mothers worry the hours spent away from home may affect their child's ability to do well in school. In the days before parent email lists and school websites, virtually all of the working mothers interviewed felt left out of the daily routine of their child's life in the classroom. They were concerned that the mothers who stayed at home had greater insights into the education process.

Some working mothers felt everyone was unhappy. Lisa B said, "The non-working moms felt they were covering for everyone, and the working parents felt guilty."

Working mothers today can leverage technology to stay connected, and many teachers send emails or weekly newsletters to keep all parents abreast of happenings in the classroom, deadlines for supplies, snacks, and projects. If you need a lot of lead time, ask your child's teacher to give you advanced warning for things that are coming up, such as a science project needing parental involvement.

What the data on grades highlights for all working mothers is the need to stay involved with children's school lives, which is easier than it used to be now that homework can be emailed home and there are more ways to stay in touch with teachers. If you work long hours, consider having your child stay for after school programs where they can get help with their homework. Some working mothers also have someone in their own home from mid to late afternoon to supervise homework. Do not feel guilty about this topic. Your child just needs to know that you care about their schoolwork.

School Isn't Always Easy

Some children will struggle and face challenges that have nothing to do with their parents' work schedules. All parents have to be involved in their child's progress; if there is a problem, seek help.

In the elementary years, 14 percent of the students reported learning disabilities. This was new territory for some of the working mothers interviewed because they had never had difficulties in school. As one mother said, "It was hard for me to be a parent of a child who struggled. I was a high achiever in school, and I did not know how to help him."

One grown child interviewed, who will be referred to as John, never heard the words "learning disability" but understood he had a "delayed ability to read." His parents knew there was a problem and had John tested. His school had a special reading program for children who were having difficulties. The children went to a separate classroom for an hour a day of additional assistance. Although the teachers tried to convince John he was lucky to be chosen, he felt very anxious. "When I had to read out loud, I could feel my hands sweating and my spine would go cold. I would practice it 100 times and then try to rush through it. Then I would look around and see if anyone was judging me. The one hour of reading was the worst."

The extra attention benefited John, and he was able to catch up. John's parents knew he hated going to the special reading class, but it was worth it. He went on to college and during our interview John described how proud he was of writing a 100-page thesis in his major.

It can be hard to watch your child struggle, but your job as parent is to support him or her, and that can mean using resources besides yourself. Working mothers know that outsourcing is often the best solution at their job, and this same philosophy needs to be used with raising children as well. It is not uncommon for children to have problems learning to read or adjusting to school. Let the experts handle the issue if they can do a better job. Stay in touch with the school and the teacher and provide whatever support is needed. Sometimes special in-school assistance is required and sometimes outside tutoring is needed. This is normal, so do not feel guilty if your child requires extra help.

Parenting Isn't Always Easy

Occasionally parents feel the need to step in, take over, and do things for their children. This may be especially true for working mothers who feel guilty or time-crunched. You may think in the moment that it is easier just to jump and do it. This is not in the best interest of your child. There are times you just need to be patient. Your efforts, and those of your child, will pay off.

Doing the work for a child does not serve him or her in the long run. One now-grown child we will call Jason described a time when he lost all interest in school and his mother helped him get his focus back on his school work. It was not a fun process for Jason (or his mother), but together they worked it out. She taught him the need to be persistent, to work hard, and to have high standards for himself. If his work was not well done initially, he needed to keep working until he got it right. It took long hours and a full school year to fix the problem, but the effort paid off.

Jason states, "There was a period between fifth and sixth grade that I just dropped out mentally. My teacher would put names on the board of students who didn't turn in homework, and my name would be up there. I was very stressed, didn't do the work, and was publicly humiliated by having my name on the board. I was in a very negative mode. I decided I had to step up and become a good student. I asked my mom to help me, and she would read my work before I turned it in. When she gave me comments, I would be really crushed. I'd cry and argue, but then I would redo it. That process was one of my least favorite experiences of growing up. This happened all through sixth grade, and by seventh grade I was up to my level. It was a huge turning point for me. Mom didn't write things for me, but she made me redo things on my own and now I am really self-sufficient. All of my academic growth happened with my mom. I was impressed with her ability to play that role."

When a child is not doing well in school, parents need to reach out and see if better study skills, support at home, or possible assistance from teachers can solve the problem. If none of these strategies work, help from other professionals may be necessary.

Everyone Can Sometimes Feel Left Out

Other results from the survey indicate that school can sometimes be difficult socially on children, whether the mother works or not. A number of questions related to the non-academic side of school. Results are broken down by gender, where most of the differences were seen. The numbers were from the general question, "Please evaluate your general school experience at each level through high school," and the choice was "Good friends."

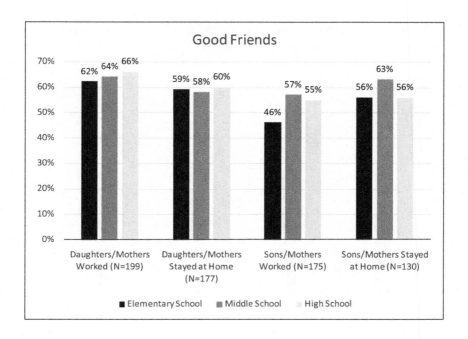

The daughters of working mothers reported having good friends more often than daughters of stay-at-home mothers, perhaps because they were more involved in sports and other school activities, which will be discussed later. Sons of working mother, however, reported lower levels of good friends than sons of stay-at-home mothers until high school, when it evened out. For all of the children, a substantial group "felt left out," with the number for daughters reaching as high as 31 percent at times during their school careers. It's a part of growing up and not connected to whether a mother works outside of the home or not.

A discouraging statistic from the survey is that approximately 20 percent of all children of felt bullied in elementary school, a number that increased to over 25 percent in middle school and then decreased below 20 percent in high school. The numbers were from the general question, "Please evaluate your general school experience at each level through high school," and the choice was "Subject to bullying."

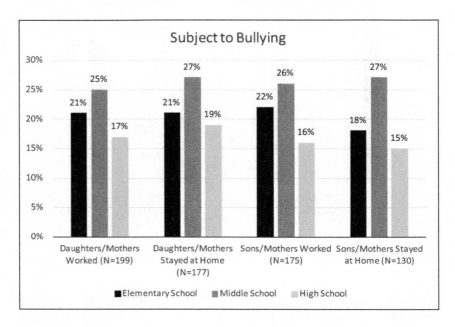

These numbers are similar to those reported on the web site of Pacer's National Bullying Prevention Center that provides statistics from the Center for Disease Control from 2013 which said 19.5 percent of high school students in the United States report being bullied at school in the past year. The site also says that 64 percent of children who were bullied did not report it. (Bullying Statistics)

Even mothers who stayed at home could not protect their children from bullies. Parents are not in the classroom with the children and rely on teachers to monitor school situations. The parents of the children in the survey at least knew where the bullies were located. Today it is even more complicated as bullying extends to online activities. All parents need to monitor their child's social situation, and working mothers can use the time at home to talk to their children about the school day and be sensitive to any issues that are troubling their children.

It All Works Out

Working mothers are their children's role models, and the problem-solving skills used at work can be applied at home. Sometimes it is okay to help out your child. Sometimes they have to learn on their own. Sometimes we all feel a little left out. It's called "life," and it's on ongoing learning experience.

One son of a working mother, Peter D, now coaches young people. He had this advice for parents. "Every little bump and bruise doesn't have a catastrophic impact. Don't put lots of barriers up for kids. Allow them the freedom to roam. The worst times were when I was forced to do things a certain way. My parents provided a buffer if I got too far off the beaten track. You need to be there, but not be there all the time."

That advice should provide peace of mind. Know that being an involved parent simply means you show genuine interest, you know what is going on with school work, and you allow your child freedom to become all that they are meant to be. The grown children acknowledge they were glad their parents were there when they needed them, and also glad that they were not there hovering all the time. Working mothers are doing a good job. Just remember that in the end the kids turn out fine.

Chapter 5

Family Time: My Mother Taught Me Family Comes First

Working mothers often feel concerned that they have less family time, and they fear it has a negative impact on their children. The survey results and the interviews reveal this is not the case. In fact, a large-scale longitudinal study reported in the April 2015 *Journal of Marriage and Family* said there was no statistically significant difference in childhood outcomes based on the amount of time spent with children. ("Does the Amount")

You have heard it said over and over, and it is true: It is not the quantity, but the quality of time that matters. Working mothers work diligently to provide quality family time. The grown children interviewed always felt family was a priority. They maintain that close family ties were a very important part of their growing up. Survey respondents provided the same feedback.

There are many ways to show your children that family comes first. The survey asked about favorite routine activities with their families, and the responses from the grown children surveyed were similar and not that surprising. Children simply liked being around their parents.

The survey participants were asked about their four favorite routine activities. The number one activity was consistent for all children. Family meals beat out other activities as a favorite nearly two to one for children of both working mothers and mothers who stayed at home.

There were subtle differences by gender that were more apparent when looking at the total "votes" for different everyday activities. The rankings are based on the total votes to be in the top four routine family activities. All events are with family.

Daughters/ Mothers Worked (N=199)	Daughters/ Mothers Stayed at Home (N=177)	Sons/Mothers Worked (N=175)	Sons/Mothers Stayed at Home (N=130)
Family meals	*Family meals*	*Family meals*	*Family meals*
Watching TV	*Watching TV (tie)*	*Watching TV*	*Watching TV*
Outdoor activities	*Outdoor activities (tie)*	*Outdoor activities*	*Outdoor activities*
Cooking/ baking	*Cooking/ baking*	*Sports (tie)*	*Sports*
Talking with parent	Talking with parent	Cooking/baking (tie)	Cooking/baking
Attending religious services	Attending religious services	Talking with parent	Attending religious services
Sports	Bedtime routine	Attending religious services	Talking with parent
Bedtime routine	Reading with parent	Bedtime routine	Bedtime routine
Reading with parent	Sports	Reading with parent	Reading with parent

The survey indicated that girls were a little more interested in cooking and baking than their brothers and boys were more interested in sports. However, the top three family activities remained the same, regardless of gender. Mothers might wonder why bedtime routines and reading or talking with parents was ranked so low, but it was all relative to the other activities. As the stories below show, families connected through all of these activities. Enjoying outdoor activities as a family is covered in another chapter.

Gather Together in the Kitchen

The heart of the home is the kitchen. Food, whether it was family dinner, baking, or breakfast, was a common way to connect and discuss the day. Working mothers can take heart; the kitchen is still the center of the home whether you are there all day or not. And for the record, you do not need dinners together every night for your children to have fond memories of family meal times.

For many people, food and family are synonymous, but it's not really about the food, it is about the conversation and the connection. What many children remember as some of the best times with their family were times spent in the kitchen or around the dinner table.

Peter E says, "Dad would cook and sit with us for our dinner and then eat later with Mom when she got home. I remember a lot of laughing." Peter also states that when the family had time, such as on vacations or weekends, dinners together were long enjoyable affairs. "We would have dinners that lasted for two and a half hours. I have always measured the quality of the dinner by how long it is. Two hours is the minimum."

Lauren H listed family dinner as her fondest memory and now incorporates the same routine in her adult life. "When we were growing up, we would sit down at the dinner table together. I know how hard that is now, even rare, because people's schedules don't align, but we did it. I learned from my parents how much of a bonding experience it can be for a couple to cook together. My boyfriend and I do that now."

For working mom Laura H, who was a lawyer, the work day started a little later and the end of the day was difficult to predict, so family breakfast was the time to connect. "When the kids were small and woke up early, we did a family breakfast during the work week. I would get up at 5:30 a.m. and shower, and then we would spend 6:00 to 7:30 a.m. together. We would make pancakes in the shape of animals and play board games. It was fluid who was cooking and who was playing, between me and my husband. I was able to spend time with my kids almost every morning, and cooking was almost always involved."

Finding the energy to cook family meals can sometimes seem impossible. It's not about the menu, it's about the company. If the children are old enough, they can help you cook. It can be wonderful bonding time. Children will often confide more of their day when they are occupied with tasks like chopping or stirring. Children like talking to their parents at the end of the day, or at the start of the day, and as long as they get a nutritious meal, it doesn't matter whether they are fed by one parent or a nanny. What does matter is for the working mother to carve out time to focus on the child, even if that child sits with you while you eat dinner at a "second shift." Any meal shared is a meal remembered.

For my children, our favorite kitchen activity was baking. I had a long commute, so the babysitter fed them dinner to be sure they had a consistent meal time. We spent many evenings talking and laughing as we measured flour and sugar and cracked eggs. Not only was baking time a fun way to discuss our days, it was a great opportunity to learn math and fractions.

Watching TV is Okay

Watching TV with the family was an activity mentioned slightly more by children of working mothers. Working mothers want to spend "quality" time with their children and sometimes feel guilty if the TV is on. Not all TV is bad, and if the programs are shared, they can be a way for a family to connect.

Matt said, "Our family was incredibly close. My parents were very intellectual and conversations were all over the place. Every night at 6:00 p.m. we watched the evening news and talked. We were not allowed to have TVs in our rooms. They wanted us to sit down together."

Nicole L remembers perfect evenings spent with her mother, Susan, in front of the television, allowing them to talk, laugh, and connect. "Mom and I both really liked old movies. On the weekend we would search for movies from the 1930s, '40s and '50s. We would watch and sing along."

Lisa B said she and her family "looked forward to Friday or Saturday nights when we had 'nests.' We would put pillows and quilts on the floor, watch movies as a family, and during the winter months have hot chocolate and popcorn." Lisa's children also mentioned Saturday and Sunday mornings when the parents sat at the kitchen table reading the paper and the children watched TV.

No one interviewed remembered the specific programs they watched with their families, but they remembered the comfort of each other's companionship.

Make Bedtime Routines Memorable

Any time of day is a good time to read with your children, but it especially makes for comforting memories at bedtime. This was commonly mentioned as a favorite activity by both the mothers and children who were interviewed.

Susan C would read to her son Justin before bed, starting with a book but then adding her own twist to the story. Catherine talked about her routine with her mother: "Every night we had a tradition at bedtime where Mom would read, tuck me in, and we would say our prayers."

Some working mothers mentioned that the time from 6:00 to 9:00 p.m. was daunting. Trying to get kids fed, bathed, and homework done in that timeframe was exhausting. Your day might seem endless, but take the time to put your children to bed—even as they get older. Younger children like to read books and hear songs. Adolescents may try to act as if they don't need you, but the end of the day is an excellent time for a teenager to start a conversation about all the issues she or he refused to talk about earlier in the evening.

Carve Out Time to Be With Your Children

Be it meals, TV time, or bedtime, carve out time to just be with your children, to let them know that family is your first priority. Working mother Judy states, "We spent a lot of energy building the nuclear family. My husband and I knew having children was the most important investment we would make as a couple. When we decided we would have children, we knew we would give everything we could to help them become healthy adults."

Judy's sentiment was also expressed by other mothers. During the years they were raising their children, their lives revolved around family. Elaine recalls, "When we were home, we were home for the kids. Our only socializing was with families with children our children's ages. We did not leave the kids with babysitters on weekends. Our house was the one where the kids always hung out. We were always home-focused, kid-focused."

For blended families, finding time to be together can be challenging, but it is doable. Kathleen and her husband worked with their ex-spouses to arrange for all three of their children to be available one night a week for family night. It was mandatory, no excuses. "Sometimes we would go out, and sometimes we would stay in. It was a night for relaxation and fun. If there were difficult issues to discuss, we saved them for another time when we could have a family meeting. On family night we would ask the kids the highest part of the week and the lowest. The kids laughed, but we did it anyway. Now that they are older, they said they always counted on those nights."

Kathleen's daughter, Alix, says, "I really liked family night. It was difficult at first, but we all really appreciated it. We still talk about it. It made an impact whether or not we appreciated it at the time."

Sarah D says, "Mothers don't need to be there all the time. Kids of working mothers are independent, but it was important to me that I got to tell my mom about my day. Mothers should make time somehow during the week to spend quality time with her kids." Anne gives this sage advice: "Listen to your children and know what is going on. Be there when they need you, even if it is just by phone."

Give Your Children One-on-One Time

Children remember when their mother focused on just them. Megan said, "When Mom took time off, it was special. I remember I asked my mom to be a chaperone on a field trip and she said yes. I wrote a note to her boss telling him it was okay for her to take the day off, like she would write a note to my teacher, and she brought it to him. I can't remember the trip or where we went but I remember that my mom gave up a day of work to spend it with me."

Lisa C always gave her sons some one-on-one time. "Every year I took each of them on a separate trip, often an extension of a business trip. The boys were four and a half years apart and at times not interested in the same things. It was more intimate to spend time one-on-one and there was less competition between the two boys." Not everyone can manage separate vacations for the children, but many of the grown children mentioned special times with parents when they were the sole focus of attention.

Be There for the Big Events

Be there for your children's important events. That is how you show family comes first. Note to working mothers: Stay-at-home mothers are not able to be there for everything either. Know what matters to your child and show your support.

Working mothers showed up for their children. Mothers who stayed at home were more often able to attend all school events, but when adding together the "attended all" and "attended the really important ones," as the chart below shows, working mothers' attendance records at teacher conferences, school events, and extracurricular events were nearly identical to mothers who stayed at home. Working mothers' attendance even surpassed stay-at-home mothers at athletic events, which will be discussed later. The answers were to general question, "Can you tell us how frequently your mother was able to attend school events and other activities?" and the choice below was for the combination of "attended all" and "attended the really important ones."

The chart is just another example that mothers who stay at home are busy as well. Even though they are "home," they have other responsibilities and may not be able to make every event, so working mothers should not feel guilty if they miss things too. Attend the events that matter to your child.

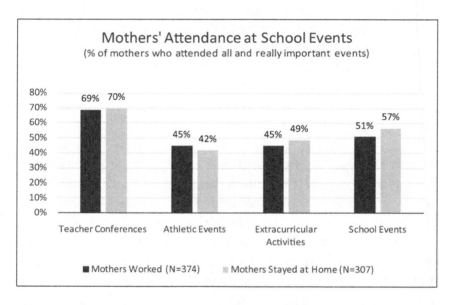

Those small celebrations during childhood are long remembered. Peter D says, "I remember my sixth grade graduation and my parents, aunt, uncle, grandparents, and godmother showed up. Now as an adult I look back, and it is surprising to me that our extended family showed up. As a kid I thought it was stupid, but now I realize it was absolutely remarkable."

Nick said, "My mom never missed a big game. She never missed a play. Sometimes she would get home at 9:00 p.m. for five days in a row, but she was always there for the important things." Anne, whose mother traveled a great deal, says, "Mom was always there when I needed her. As long as a mother is at the ballet recital, explains puberty, goes prom dress shopping, and can talk about how to ask a guy out, then the child doesn't mind at all if the mother works."

Provide a Role Model of Loving Relationships

For those working mothers who are married, your example of making it work makes an impact on your children whether you (or they) realize it or not. The teamwork you display is a good role model. Sharing household duties, organizing who does what, arranging childcare when needed, taking part in school events and outside activities, and relying on each other to make the family operate smoothly shows your priority is your family.

Susan D says, "My husband and I met in business school so he knew he was getting into a dual career marriage. He was always supportive. He was in it from the beginning." Her husband always played a very active role with their children, especially in sports. With three children, they had to divide and conquer often. Her daughter Maggie says, "My parents had a great relationship with each other, which is rare in America. They were good role models." Peter D stated, "The biggest carryover I have is that my parents provided me with a really fantastic example of a strong marriage. I didn't realize how awesome it was until I grew up."

Parents who are divorced also have the opportunity to provide role models for their children. In many cases, a second marriage turns out to be very successful, even if the children are not always accepting in the beginning. When Kathleen met and married her second husband, he had two children from a prior marriage. Kathleen believes that one of the benefits of the second marriage to the children was, "We taught them what a loving relationship can be between people."

It can be especially hard for working parents to make time for their own relationship, but it is a good investment of time. Your marriage is a role model for your children. How you and your spouse treat each other will be a template for your children's own marriages.

Make Sure Children Know Their Extended Family

Mothers want their children to know their grandparents, aunts, uncles, and cousins. Families that were separated by distance had to work hard to be sure their children had time with their relatives.

Pattie wanted her son Chris to be connected to her family. "My parents were the patriarch and matriarch of the family, and Chris respects them more than anyone in the world. They were great role models. I come from a family of seven kids, and we each think we are our parents' favorite. Chris spent several summers there. My extended family is huge and I wanted him to know them. He was an only child and his cousins taught him how to have siblings. His aunts and uncles taught him the value of an extended family."

Kathleen and her husband both come from large families, and she admits it has its up sides and down sides. "Extended family is a big part of my husband's and my life. Sometimes it is challenging, but it is the fabric of who we are as a family. The family is all so opinionated. It provided a strong safety net for the kids. You knew you were never alone. Sometimes there are a whole lot of people in your stuff." There were times her daughter Alix felt more comfortable talking to one of Kathleen's sisters than her own mother, and Kathleen was okay with that. Kathleen felt it was good that Alix had other adults in her life she could turn to.

Working mothers have so little time, it is easy to just stay in their own world. Children, however, benefit from seeing their extended family and getting to know their relatives. As we will see later, grandparents are often mentioned as mentors by the grown children, so making the effort to see them is worth it.

Enjoy Your Children

Weekends are a time for working parents to catch up with the family, and the children interviewed had many stories of running errands with parents on weekends. Time with your children does not have to be complicated or filled with any special activity. While you are driving around with your children, talk—and listen. Some of the best times to talk to a child one-on-one are in the car. Understand what sports games and events are important to your child and make sure you get there.

Working mothers aren't always available to drive during the week, but many mothers mentioned volunteering for carpools on weekends. Even if their own child was not very talkative, they could listen to the conversation in the backseat and get caught up.

Teach your children the value of family. What it takes is a working mother's most valuable commodity—time. Have family meals, if not every night, then one night a week. If you can't make it home in time for dinner, then try to be there to put the children to bed. Even teenagers like the opportunity to talk about their day or any problems they might be having.

It boils down to staying connected. That's what children need. Give them the security of knowing you care about what goes on in their lives. Show them family really does come first.

Chapter 6

Downtime: My Mother Taught Me How to Enjoy Life

Busy working parents often fall into a routine where they just plow through the day and check things off the list. Working mothers also feel pressure to educate their children and teach them rules. You are instilling in them good values and a strong work ethic. Equally important is demonstrating how to enjoy life. Combining the chores that need to be done along with teaching children to enjoy the little things in life is good for both children and mothers. The grown children surveyed and interviewed had fond memories of the simple things they did with their parents and of just having fun as a family.

When working mothers were asked what they would do differently, many of them said they wished they had spent more quiet time with their children. Kathleen said, "I always made sure we were scheduled to do a lot of things. I wish I had planned more downtime, more relaxation." Joanie echoed that sentiment; "I wish I had less of the practical 'must have' and more of the 'nice to have' moments like reading and board games." Susan D said, "I wish I had slowed down a little and spent more quiet time."

Make Simple Events Fun

Like most working mothers, Susan G used weekends to catch up on chores and Saturday morning was set aside to clean the house. Her daughter Danielle now includes those times among her favorite memories. Danielle talked about "helping" her mother, even when she was four or five years old, saying, "My mom would put on Bruce Springsteen, turn it up loud, and we would dance and sing while cleaning." Susan took a task that most women dislike and turned it into a fun event. Not only did Danielle list Saturday morning housecleaning as one her favorite recollections of childhood, she says, "Every time I hear Bruce Springsteen, I smile."

A number of children mentioned that they enjoyed going to the grocery store with their mothers. David B has warm memories of accompanying his mother Toni while she did her weekly food shopping. This was usually on a school night, which made it even more exciting for David to be out with his mother. David would ride in the cart and he says he tried to be very good so his mother would give him the candy bar she promised him if he behaved. You don't have to make elaborate plans. Simple fun can happen anytime—even at the supermarket.

I loved grocery shopping with my daughter. I would come home from work, pick her up, and drive back to the store rather than stopping on my way home and shopping by myself. Strolling up and down the aisles with Sarah riding in the cart, I would take products off the shelf and point out words. She swears she learned how to read in the grocery store. It is still one of my favorite places, and I enjoy seeing the children in the carts and watching the interaction with their mothers.

Working mothers need to be careful they do not let their partners have all the fun. Several mothers mentioned that her spouse got to be the "good" guy while she was the "tough" guy. Elaine says, "My husband was really good at sitting on the floor and playing with the kids. He's always been the 'fun' parent and I've always been the 'serious' parent." Maybe that is your natural personality, but even if you are the stricter parent, be sure you have your share of the fun times with your children. You deserve it.

Share What You Love With Your Children

Share whatever you love with your children. It will feel much less like work and more like fun to incorporate simple joys. Use time at home on work nights or weekends for music, dance, or art.

Sylvia, her husband, daughter, and son all enjoy music. While they were cooking and cleaning up in the kitchen, the entire family would sing and dance. One of them would pick a popular song and then they would take turns making up new lyrics.

Rebecca talked enthusiastically about the ways her imaginative parents entertained them on the weekends. She knew her parents had demanding jobs running their advertising business, but on weekends the focus was on the family. "Whenever we did things, they made sure it was really fun. They are pretty creative people. They were very attentive and we all had fun." A big event for the entire family was Halloween when they hosted the biggest party in the neighborhood and set up a haunted house in the garage.

For those of us who are better at appreciating art than creating it, we can still provide creative opportunities for our children. When I moved to Boston from New York, I was delighted to find that Boston had a wonderful museums and performing arts organizations that provided programs for children of all ages. Many weekends, especially during the long winter months, we were at one museum or another. I was touched recently when my son Paul, instead of buying me a gift for my birthday, donated money in my name to the Museum of Science to remind me of all the great times we had there.

Birthdays Are to Be Celebrated

Feeling loved and receiving attention is always important, and especially on birthdays. Parents may sometimes think these parties are just another "project" to be handled, but to the children interviewed, they were a visible sign their parents cared about them. Many children mentioned birthdays as a time they remember being the center of attention and feeling loved.

Josh says one of his favorite memories is a birthday party when his parents set up the basement so every child could built his or her own rocket ship. Josh says, "I have a very positive memory of my childhood. I remember laughing and smiling a lot while playing around the house."

Beth's parents went all out for birthdays. "My mom always made the biggest deal about our birthdays. My brother and I were born twelve days apart and it was not a birth day, it was a birth month. We had four parties for my birthday— one at school, one for the family, one for my friends, and a joint one with my brother." Clearly this family knew how to celebrate.

However you decide to celebrate, and no matter when the birthday falls, allowing each child to feel special is worth the effort. Birthdays come just once a year and are an opportunity to create a wonderful memory for your child. You don't have to do crafts, and you can buy a cake from the store. It's about the celebration of your child's special day and to have the child be reminded how much you love him or her.

Teach Children to Enjoy Themselves Outdoors

Outdoor activities with the family was ranked as the second favorite activity on the survey by children of both working and stay-at-home mothers. No matter where you live, you and your children can experience the great outdoors and have fun outside.

Gay and her husband raised their children to appreciate the outdoors. Gay says, "My husband is a fifth-generation Texas rancher, and his family had a large ranch in South Texas. A lot of weekends were spent with the children on the ranch. Our kids had a great outdoor experience growing up. They were taught how to ride and shoot guns. We taught them about plants and wildlife." Ben remembers, "We were outside the whole time. There were so many things to do as a kid. It was great to have the freedom to explore."

Several of the families in the northern parts of the country mentioned skiing as a way to get the family outdoors. Marcia said, "When there were double chair lifts, you had ten minutes to sit and talk to your child uninterrupted and undistracted. You could talk about challenging things and then ski down and decide whether to continue the conversation." She went on, "The ski trips were so nice to have because it was built-in alone time. The kids also got a lifelong sport."

Megan's family owned a blueberry farm. A big part of her childhood was outside. "We grew all of our vegetables for the entire year and froze them. We had animals—sheep and pigs—and when the babies were born I would cuddle the babies while my parents were dealing with the mother. Now I look back and wonder how many kids get a chance to do that. It was wonderful."

When Megan was a teenager, she became restless and wanted to leave the rural life. She now works in a city. She said, "I wanted to leave the small town where I grew up and couldn't wait to get away. Recently I asked my mom to send me some pictures from my childhood and she sent me a picture I love—one where we are in a sleigh, riding through the blueberry field."

Judy and her husband raised their two daughters in San Francisco, and daughter Deborah loved walking with her parents to the park. "There was a park close to our house. In San Francisco there are a lot of hills, and long walls separated the residential side from the park. We got to walk on one side of the wall and hold hands with my parents on the other side." In this case it was not just playing in the park, but the walk and the comfort of holding a parent's hand that made the excursion special. In all the examples the interviewees provided, the outdoors were coupled with good family memories.

Lisa C used to go stir crazy during the winter. When she lived in New York and then Chicago with her husband and their two sons, she looked for ways to get outdoors, even in the cold weather. She came up with the idea of picnics as a way to get outside. She explains it as, "Picnics—roof top, park, full moon, beach, and car picnics. We would set up a little spot. It was fun to be outside in a place where it was easier to be inside." In Chicago they would go up to the roof top for hot cocoa. "The full moon picnic, even in winter, was a sense of celebration. The car picnics were a way of making it fun to eat in the car when traveling."

Not every child can be raised on a ranch, farm, or even in a suburb, but parks are everywhere. Near my home there is a bike path, and after work I see parents riding with their children, families walking dogs, and parents running while their children ride bikes. Finding time after work to get some exercise with your child is good for both of you. If it is too dark by the time you get home or finish dinner, find a place in town or on a school campus with lighted paths and just go for a walk.

If you can't do it during the week, plan to get outside on the weekend. Turn your electronic devices off. Sometimes it is easier to get a child to talk about his or her day when you are not sitting across a table and are away from the distractions of TVs, computers, or mobile phones. Get outside some way and play.

Find Ways to Make a Day Special

Working mothers can get in a rut and look at each day as a marathon to finish instead of an opportunity to have fun with their children. You need to break out of your routine and shake things up from time to time. And children love surprises.

Judy and her husband made a game of taking their daughters to new places without allowing them to vote on the destination. Their daughter, Deborah, remembers "Take Me" days when her parents would just tell Deborah and her sister what to bring and take them to a surprise location. "It was special time as a family. We did fun and interesting things together and there were little surprises involved." The visits ranged from the zoo to "the ultimate—skipping school to go to Disneyland."

Lauren J remembers days alone with each of her parents. "My mother and I had special days we would spend together doing cultural things. I had 'Lauren and Daddy Days' too. We would go to movies, get ice cream, or go to amusement parks and go on amazing roller coasters." Since Lauren and her brother were seven years apart, her parents used the time alone with her to do things that appealed to her at her age.

When children are different ages, it can be hard to include them in the same events, so parents need to adjust. Laura H said, "My boys are 'all boy' and have sports on 24/7 and go to a lot of sports games. My husband and his father had Patriots tickets and took our sons. When our younger son, Nick, was around four he was too young to go, so he and I did something special to include him. We went to the grocery store to buy food, we watched the game on TV, and made the meal that we served when the others returned. It made him feel part of the game."

When my daughter was horseback riding every Saturday, she did not want me and her brother to sit around and watch her. It was a long drive to and from the farm and I hated to have my son spend all of his Saturday in the car driving his sister to her events. We got into a routine where Paul and I had a nice lunch together at a country diner, eating outside on a picnic table in the good weather. Suddenly Saturday had been turned from Sarah's riding day to the day Paul and I had a private lunch. We needed to eat anyway, so we made it a special occasion.

Working mothers can find the time to do something unexpected with their children once in a while too. It is good for children to realize life is not the same every day. Create your own family adventures. As you can see from these examples, children do not need anything elaborate, they simply need to feel special.

It may seem unimaginable for busy working mothers to just slow down and have fun with their children, but it can be done. Family life shouldn't be as well orchestrated as the business world. The house does not need to be perfect, and the projects will get done eventually. Children love to come along with parents wherever the parents go. The chores that working mothers think of as just another responsibility in their already full lives are adventures to their children. Include your child as you work around the house or run errands. Working mothers are used to getting a lot of things done because their lives are so busy. However, sometimes the best thing to do is—nothing. Relax and enjoy your children and enjoy life.

Chapter 7

Holidays: My Mother Taught Me to Honor Traditions

Creating memories and honoring traditions happen in everyday life. As we have already seen, movie night with the family or a trip to the grocery store with Mom became lasting memories. Many of the grown children incorporate the traditions from their childhood into their adult lives.

Tradition and ritual can be very comforting and can come from anything. Nearly all of the working mothers interviewed felt holidays are a time to pass on traditions, to get together with family and friends, and to make lasting memories. Mothers know holidays provide a unique opportunity to create special remembrances for their children, so although holidays added extra work to their already full schedules, the mothers looked forward to recreating the rituals of their own childhood.

Holidays Are Special

Children love occasions to celebrate and the children of both working mothers and stay-at-home mothers listed holidays as their second favorite special family activity, right after vacations. The question asked in the survey was, "What were your four favorite special family activities?" The numbers below reflect the number one choice.

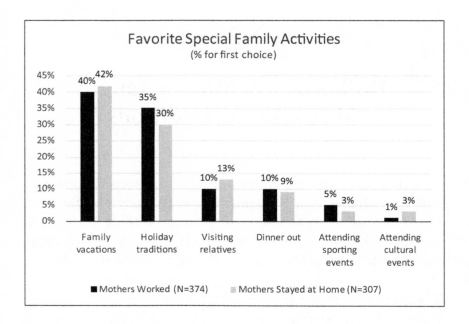

While all children loved holidays, it appears children of working mothers liked them even more than children of mothers who stayed at home. This could be because working mothers spent more time at home during these periods, which was part of what made holidays so special.

For many families, Thanksgiving is the major holiday to gather, and food is the star. It is a time to extend beyond the nuclear family and expose children to the joy—and imperfection—of family and friends. For working mothers and their children, taking a break from the daily routine is a welcome respite, even if there is "work" to do.

Susan D says, "Thanksgiving was our big holiday, and I always cooked. Everyone came to me on Thanksgiving. We had local people and friends from out of town." Big gatherings provide the opportunity for lasting memories and the embedding of traditions.

Susan's son Peter remembers it the same way. "My mother takes Thanksgiving very seriously—it is bigger than Christmas at our house—and fifteen to seventeen people for dinner was the norm. We had family and close connections with other families who are like blood relatives. Sometimes there was some contention, like all families, but it is to be expected. My family is very aggressive and we just let it all out!" Daughter Maggie listed Thanksgiving as one of her favorite memories; she said, "Thanksgiving is a big deal in our family. I loved helping Mom cook. She is a fantastic cook, and I like to cook now as well."

Sharing what you love with your children is important. Anne says, "For Thanksgiving, my mom would only use vegetables she grew herself in the garden. She cooked for three days leading up to the dinner. She had enough food for thirty to forty people even though there were only fifteen or sixteen of us."

Many children have a favorite dish that they look forward to. Sometimes the fact that it only happens once a year at Thanksgiving is what makes it so special. Chris's family still gets together at his grandparents' farm in Mississippi, where food is the main event. "We have the standard Thanksgiving food—turkey, ham, mashed potatoes. One of my aunts makes sweet potatoes covered in marshmallow, which I love." Special Thanksgiving food can be a comforting memory for a child, young or grown, any time of year.

Carving out time for tradition and making memories is important. With the way schedules fall for December holidays, gathering in November for Thanksgiving often is the best time for many families to get together. Lauren J has fond memories. "We were usually at our home for Thanksgiving with lots of family—aunts, uncles, cousins. We would be cooking and football would be on during the food preparation. There was a kids' table and a grown-ups' table. At Christmas we could be scattered, but at Thanksgiving we were all together."

That's what makes these occasions stand out—making special foods and the effort to all be together. Even with "feisty" families, the children (and the mothers) look at Thanksgiving as a day of fun, with food, friends, and family.

For many years, my children and I spent Thanksgiving in New Orleans with my sister and her family. My sister was a working mother of two daughters and traveled even more than I did, so finding time to see each other was difficult. Since we both wanted to be in our own homes for Christmas, Thanksgiving was a perfect time to plan to be together. My sister is a great cook, but what I remember about these trips is not the food. It was the hours we had to catch up on each other's lives and watching our children run around and have fun together.

A number of the women interviewed had to work the day after Thanksgiving, but that did not diminish the pleasure of the holiday or the memories created. Taking the time to celebrate Thanksgiving is worth all the hours of preparation. All during the year, life can be hectic and it is good to take time out, especially on this holiday, to reconnect with those you care about. The conversations and caring you share with the other adults can be just as important as the food and fun you are giving to your children.

Another thing many working mothers love about Thanksgiving is no presents. You may have to juggle travel or additional meal planning, but you don't have to worry about gifts. That is something working mothers are thankful for.

Celebrate More, Stress Less

For many working mothers, the long holiday season brings both joy and pressure to provide the perfect holiday for their family. While all mothers feel this stress, it can be even harder on working mothers who may be faced with year-end projects, budgets, or closing deadlines. Despite their lack of time, the working mothers interviewed loved the holidays. Those who could manage it took time off to allow them extra time with their family.

Vicki says, "Holidays were so much fun, talking, being together. I always took off the week between Christmas and New Year and we'd spend the time cooking and doing puzzles." Her daughter Lauren also remembers holidays as being special. "Mom has always been the ringleader, and she brought so much magic to the holidays. Even though we are grown up, she still puts out cookies for Santa. We would always gather a lot of the family together and sure, there were the typical conflicts and arguments once in a while, but it was always fun."

Holidays are a time to gather. Joanie and her husband have a large, extended family and both sides of the family had a tradition to get together Christmas Eve. "Christmas is a huge, huge deal. We have a video of every Christmas since our oldest was born. We have not had a single Christmas without all three of the girls being home. We may not all be together this year and I am in tears just thinking about it." Her daughter Susannah likes that Christmas holds a lot of traditions. She enjoyed going to her grandmother's house, where the cousins would do Secret Santa. As they have grown, they have developed new traditions. Susannah loved Christmas Eve and the fun of getting all dressed up to go be with family.

It does not matter what your traditions are, the point is to take a breather from work and enjoy. You may enjoy getting dressed up, visiting, and entertaining during holidays. You may choose to celebrate in an altogether different way.

Elaine used the holidays to relax. "We took off the week between Christmas and New Year's, which we call 'pajama week.' We didn't leave the house and just made gingerbread houses and baked cookies. We ate junk food and watched movies." Her son Matt remembers, "Every year Mom would buy us each an ornament that represented our year. For example, one year when I had a job in a kitchen store she bought me a chef ornament. When I went to the University of Wisconsin, she bought me an ornament from Wisconsin. Each child's ornaments were packed in a separate box and each year we got to decide whether we wanted to hang them up. She still has them."

Traditions and memories are what the grown children are grateful for, a gift you can give to your family. Many enjoyed the holiday ballet *The Nutcracker*. Susan D remembers the pleasure of watching daughter Maggie dance. "Maggie had always done ballet and she was in *The Nutcracker*. As she got older, she graduated to bigger and bigger roles." Not everyone was a dancer, but many of the children who were interviewed had the tradition of attending this famous holiday classic. Rory remembers it as one of her favorite times. "We would go to *The Nutcracker* every year. My mother, grandmother, and I would get all dressed up, go to tea, and then go to *The Nutcracker*."

Working mothers all handled holiday preparations differently. Since presents had to be mailed to my family who were all out of town, I finished most of my shopping by Thanksgiving and sent them off. Holiday cards were mailed shortly after, and the house was fully decorated. That left me with the entire month of December to take my children to *The Nutcracker*, a Christmas concert, and holiday parties. Even Christmas Eve was relaxing because when Santa came to our house he did not believe in wrapping presents, he just laid them out on either side of the tree for my children.

My friend Anne has the exact opposite approach to Christmas. She believes it would not be Christmas if she were not wrapping presents late on Christmas Eve and rarely gets her cards out before January.

It does not matter how you handle the holidays. Do whatever works for you, your family, and your work schedule. Simply knowing you are creating special memories with your children that they will take with them throughout their lives can make any time you spend together magical. Perhaps the most important thing to remember is to relax.

Holidays Don't Need to Be Perfect

The working mothers interviewed were used to doing things well, and holidays were no exception. They often had unrealistic expectations for themselves and sometimes had to remind themselves of the meaning of the holidays.

Laura H admits to "doing" Christmas to the point of causing everyone lots of stress. She said, "I spend two months getting ready, and it drives the boys crazy." Elaine had to realize she could not manage the holidays the way she did projects at work. She said, "I like my gingerbread house and cookies perfect, and it took me years to realize Jessica could have her own house and dough and make her own. We had this all figured out, and then the boys came along and messed them up. We decided we could have a village of gingerbread houses and everyone could have his or her own."

Susan G was brought up in an observant Jewish home. She and her husband Jim wanted their two children to experience the value of living in a Jewish community. Since Jim was raised in a secular Jewish family, Susan knew if she was going to pass on these values to her children, she had to take the lead. Normally, during the Seder the father would lead the prayers while the mother did the cooking, but since Jim had no experience leading the prayers, Susan did both. She found this frustrating at times but daughter Danielle did not seem to notice her mother's concerns about getting it perfect. Danielle enjoyed holiday times and remembers they would read the prayers at Passover. Susan continues honoring these Jewish traditions, which Danielle appreciates. "Mom picks out a modern-day story of someone being courageous and promoting social justice."

The holidays, and life, are not about perfection. It's about being present. You can honor the holidays for your family without having the food and decorations look like they do on television or in the magazines. Finding the balance of what is right for you is key.

Working mother Polly learned that lesson from her children. When Livey and Mary were in high school, Polly was working extremely long hours at her job in New York City and then had to commute to their home in the suburbs. Polly told her children she was too busy to buy and decorate a tree one year, especially since they were going to see family in Providence for Christmas. However, her children did not think it was Christmas without their own tree and secretly took the matter into their own hands.

Livey got a tree and managed to get it home on his bike since he did not yet have a driver's license. Mary decorated the tree after her cheerleading practice. Polly was overwhelmed when she came home and saw it. She believes her children knew better than she did how much the tree symbolized the Christmas spirit.

Many of the children and mothers talked about making gingerbread houses, and my children and I loved creating the houses each year too. Even now, when my children and I live in three different cities, we share pictures of the gingerbread houses we each decorate, and it continues to bond us together.

Working mothers have high standards at work, and lowering them at home is easier intellectually than in practice. But there are many ways to have fun holidays with your children without putting too much pressure on yourself. If you want to make gingerbread houses, they can be purchased preassembled and you can add your own candy by putting it on with a can of pre-made white frosting. It's about the fun of doing the project together.

Stop thinking you have to do it all yourself. Presents can be wrapped by the store where you purchased them. Holiday cards can be done electronically or mailed by online service companies. Full holiday dinners can be picked up at many grocery stores. Continue to do the things you love to do, but don't feel you have to do everything.

Children simply want time with their mother, and they want their mother to be happy. That's what you want for your children too. Don't create extra stress for yourself or your family at a time that should be joyful and relaxing. Put on some music and spend some time together. Ask your children what they most want to do. You may be surprised they would rather watch a movie with you, bake some cookies, or play a board game. The holidays are all about making memories together. These are the traditions your children will cherish and honor in their adult lives as well.

Chapter 8

Vacations: My Mother Taught Me Vacations Matter

Family vacations were the favorite special family activity of children with working mothers and children with mothers who stayed at home. As the chart in the last chapter showed, vacations topped the list as the most favorite special family activity. It was listed as number one by 40 percent of children whose mothers worked and 42 percent of children whose mother stayed at home.

The grown children interviewed found vacations were a time to explore new places with their parents. For working mothers, it was precious time with their children. When families were able to travel, the mother was liberated from her home duties as well and had a rare experience of freedom from all her responsibilities. Working mothers need to make vacations a priority. They are good for you and your children.

Take a Break

Oxford Economics released a study in February 2014 stating 42 percent of American workers do not use all of their paid time off, leaving an average of 8.1 days unused ("An Assessment"). One credit card company even aired a television commercial where incredulous children cited this statistic. Clearly the point was children want more time with their parents.

Joanie came from a family that never took a vacation because if her electrician father didn't work, he didn't get paid. When

Joanie had her own family, vacations with her husband and their three daughters were a new experience and a respite from all her obligations at home. "I absolutely loved hearing them laugh on vacation. When we were at home, we worked long hours and I had to keep the trains running the next day, the next week, and the next month. On vacation, I didn't have those responsibilities. I was the one behind the camera taking the pictures. I could watch them and play with them in ways I couldn't do at home."

Joanie's daughter Caitlyn remembers vacations in a simpler way. "We had lots of great vacations growing up. We went to family camps. It was fun just to have time together. We all appreciated it, even at our young ages. We knew my parents didn't get to do this when they were growing up. Our basement is lined with pictures of the vacations." Caitlyn's last point is one mentioned by many of the children. Having pictures of the vacations and holidays allowed the families to relive the experiences even after they were all back to their busy lives.

It may be hard to stop being the one taking all the pictures, but be sure to have someone else take group photos so you can be in some of the pictures too. Now that most mobile phones have built-in cameras, it is easy to do. Take as many fun shots of you with your children as you can. The children will enjoy the pictures and you will have an archive of your vacations together.

Susan D has wonderful memories of vacations with her husband and their children. "My most cherished memories are vacations where we got away. My parents rented a house on a lake in New Hampshire. It forced us to take a step back from our busy lives. We swam, fished, went boating, and drove around the White Mountains." Her daughter Maggie remembers, "We had lots of time to be together. We went to the lake and we all had fun."

Notice that a vacation does not have to be elaborate. Simple times at a camp or lake create special times and wonderful memories. The break from the normal routine lets you all recharge and lets your children see you in a more relaxed state of mind. You don't have to have an agenda. Let each day take its course and let the memories take hold.

Lisa B and her husband found time every summer to get away with their children and visit with family. "We went away to the beach for one month every summer. We were still working, but we tag-teamed our days off and days working. We were near family during this time. My sister rented the house next door and we were near my parents. We just picked up and went away as a family."

Both of Lisa's children remember this as one of their favorite times. Lisa's daughter Laura said, "Every summer we would go to a beach for a month with our family. We did this for ten years." Her brother Daniel remembers, "We would go to the beach for four or five weeks during the summer. We rented a cottage on the sound, where it was quiet. Our extended family—aunts, uncles, cousins, grandparents—would all visit." Details might be slightly different as each family member recalls the past, but the memories of the pleasurable times they had as a family were the same.

Susan G's daughter Danielle remembers having some great outings camping and hiking. Her father grew up hiking, but her mother did not. "One of my favorite trips was to Acadia National Park in Maine, where we rented a cute little cabin. We ate lobster ice cream, which was disgusting. On most of the hikes, Mom would tell Dad he was too ambitious about what we could do." Sounds like a typical family hike, but Danielle listed it as one of her favorite memories.

Susan C has always had her own consulting business that required a lot of travel. For Susan, the lines between business travel and vacation travel blurred. She started bringing her son Justin with her on business trips when he was just six months old. He accompanied her all over the United States, Puerto Rico, Europe, and the Caribbean, with a babysitter in tow when he was young. Susan did not treat business travel as a liability of her job that kept her away from her only child, but as an opportunity for them to share together the many wonderful places she visited. Other working mothers talked about taking children with them on business trips, especially as they got older and childcare was not as much of an issue, and extending trips to allow time to explore with the child.

In today's fully connected world, it is harder than ever to completely get away from work, but working mothers need to try the best they can to focus on their children when they are on vacation. One working mother I know has her work email deleted from her phone while she is on vacation. If you can't do that, set aside one time during the day to check in and focus the rest of your energy on your family. You all deserve it.

Family Retreats Are a Way to Reconnect

Family vacations weren't just about seeing new places or things, they were about seeing each other in new roles. Working mother Myra said, "Every summer we took a family camping trip. We went to the Rockies, the Great Lakes, Glacier, Yosemite, etc. Of course my idea of camping was two days of camping and one day in a hotel."

Her daughter Holly said, "Camping trips were the big family vacation. One year we drove from Chicago to Spokane and we stopped at national parks along the way. As kids, we hoped it would rain because then we would stay in a motel with a bed that you could put quarters into and feel its 'magic fingers.' We had one giant old tent that had been sewn up when it had been attacked by a bear (or so my parents said). There was always a big dispute on where to put it up, and one year we put it in a gulch and when the rain came, it was all washed up. We never went to a fancy campsite so we had to clear the campsite and collect wood for a fire. We never actually spent more than two nights in one place because we were on our way to see the next park or monument."

Holly continues, "Looking back now as a parent, I find it incredible that my parents went to all that work. We went to places like Glacier, Acadia, and Lake Superior. The places were stunningly beautiful. We would bike, swim, and maybe get a boat. We had to do it all together. I have tried to recreate this with my own family to allow them to experience the national parks. My parents opened this entire world up to me."

Holly's sister Jean had a similar description. "We would pack up the station wagon and drive out west to one of the national parks or up to Canada. It was the best low budget vacation our parents could think of. We had a gigantic tent with a hole in it from a bear. Mom will tell you that every few days we stopped at a motel so we could shower and clean up, but we kids liked the camping part best."

Myra's children have their own families now, and they try to have vacations all together when they can. Myra says, "This summer we are renting a big house in Tahoe. Every three years or so we take time to get together for two weeks."

One of Toni's best memories is taking her two boys on an extended driving vacation when she was an associate at her law firm. "When I was still an associate, I took an extra month vacation and took the summer off to drive across country with the boys. My husband was teaching at Michigan for the summer and we met up with him there after stopping off at Niagara Falls. We then went on to California and drove home."

Toni's sons David and Jeffrey also cited the trip as a favorite memory. David says, "My mother took off eight weeks so that she could take my brother and me on a road trip throughout the country. It was a big deal for my mother to take a leave of absence from her busy law practice. She had to do all of the driving since my brother and I were too young to drive. We went to St. Louis, Colorado, Buffalo, San Francisco (where my mother had an American Bar Association meeting), Canada, etc. It was a fabulous trip."

Vicki and her daughter Lauren described the same vacation as one of their favorite memories. In Lauren's words, "We were lucky to go to Hawaii, and one of my favorite times was when we were snorkeling in an out-of-the way place. Suddenly there was a squeaking noise and we were surrounded by fifty dolphins who were swimming around us and playing with us. We all went crazy." Vicki's version added, "It was an experience of a lifetime to see this kind of event in nature, and we had shared it all together. It was wonderful."

Not everyone can take months off or drive across country, but getting away and seeing and learning new things together lets children and their parents see each other in a different light. Even disasters like the tent getting washed away can be a bonding experience.

I took my children on a number of short trips to cities I had visited on business and always wanted to see as a tourist. We did long weekends in San Francisco; Washington, DC; San Antonio; San Diego; Seattle; Vancouver; and Montreal. The place and the activity do not matter. We laughed just as much when it rained for our entire week of vacation on Cape Cod. It's the time off and the time together that make the impression.

International Travel Exposes Children to Different Cultures

Some parents took their children overseas to see different cultures or to visit family living abroad. Even working mothers who did not have such opportunities encouraged their children to take advantage of international educational opportunities.

Sylvia says, "Both of our kids traveled extensively—Europe, South America, and the Caribbean. We believed this made them better, well-rounded citizens of the world. Evan even studied in France at the Sorbonne when he was in high school."

There were many ways to see other countries. Rick remembers that one summer his parents arranged a house swap with a family in Geneva, Switzerland. "It was a period of concentrated time together with my sisters and mom when she was not working."

Laura H was born in Munich, Germany, while her parents were in the foreign service. She lived in several countries, attending French schools throughout, and didn't relocate permanently to the United States until high school. To Laura it was natural that she would travel with her boys because it was the way she had been raised. As a family they would go to London for a long weekend, which is actually a shorter flight from Boston than to Los Angeles. Laura's mother now lives in Puerto Rico, and every Thanksgiving the family would go there and the boys would take friends. "We would sit outside, have long meals and conversations." It wasn't just international travel, it was a way to see family.

Nicole A grew up in St. Helena, California, where she was educated to be bilingual in Spanish. Her parents owned vineyards in California and Oregon and traveled frequently to generate interest in their wines. "As I got older, they took me with them as often as possible, and it sparked my interest in living in Europe." Nicole got her wish and now lives in Spain with her Italian husband and their daughter and son. Mother Nancy says of her daughter's family, "They have an amazingly rich cultural life."

Susan F moved her family to London when a job opportunity presented itself, and it allowed her to get her two daughters into an international atmosphere. Susan said, "When I was in my early twenties, I had lived for six years in Brussels and knew how much I had benefitted from being able to travel to different countries and meet people whose backgrounds were dissimilar from my own. We lived in a small English town while I commuted into London, and the girls went to an international school. As a family we traveled to Rome for the Thanksgiving holiday, France in the summer, and the Netherlands in the spring. To this day my older daughter, in eighth grade when we moved, remains close friends with her London school buddies who came from all over the world."

My own children's first "international" experiences were eating in Italian, Chinese, and Thai restaurants and going to international exhibits at the Boston Children's Museum. Later, I took my children to countries where I thought it would be easy to travel to with children: Canada, England, France, and Italy. At this point, both of them are much better traveled than I am, having studied abroad while in college and traveled overseas for both business and pleasure.

Working mothers know our children will work in a diverse environment, and the more chances we give them to be exposed to people with different backgrounds and points of view, the more successful they will be. If the family budget does not allow for a trip abroad, expose them to the multiple cultures within our own country. Recently one mother with school-age children told me she makes sure her children participate in all of the ethnic events their schools offer. Her opinion was that over the years, these events are providing an excellent education on different cultures, even if the children think it is all about the food and music.

Vacations provide a wonderful experience working mothers can share with their children. Children love to have learning experiences with you. Make it a priority to take vacations together. Take plenty of photos. Don't just keep the pictures in digital format, print some out and frame them to have around the house. Your experiences with your children do not need to be perfect and in fact often make better stories when they are not seamless. It is the shared experiences that are special. Do not be part of the statistic of people who do not take advantage of all their vacation days. Show your family that vacations matter.

Chapter 9

Mentors: My Mother Taught Me That I Need Many Mentors

Children have many connections in their daily lives with other adults, and some of these people have a profound influence on them. These adults provide a great deal of support, which varies by their roles in the children's lives.

The grown children in both the survey and interviews had lives that had been enriched by teachers, family members, family friends, and coaches who mentored them and provided strong role models. The African proverb "it takes a village to raise a child" was alive and well in these families, and many of the grown children have wonderful memories of their "village."

Teachers Are a Positive Influence

In the survey, grown children were asked, "Were there adults other than your parents who had a significant positive influence on you? If so, how did they impact you?" The choices below were for "Teacher."

Both children with stay-at-home mothers and working mothers listed "teacher" most often as the adult, other than their parents, who gave them confidence, taught them skills, broadened their perspective, and provided a positive role model. Daughters of working mothers especially noted the skills taught by teachers.

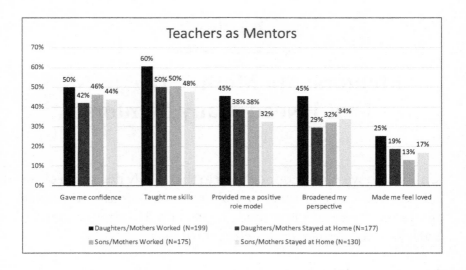

These statistics are interesting but it is the stories of the children interviewed that bring them to life. The strong feelings described by the children should not surprise anyone, but what was surprising was the depth of the memories of these teachers decades after the children had left their classroom. Usually the memories had nothing to do with the subject officially being taught.

The teachers and principals remembered were the ones who stepped in to help when children needed a little more support at certain times in their lives. Megan remembers when she transferred from public to Catholic school, "I cried every day. Sister Mary terrified me at first, but she made me realize I could do the work. It was a big turning point in my school career."

Sister Mary helped Megan overcome her fears in a way her parents could not, because as a teacher she was there in the moment and knew exactly what Megan was facing. She was able to give Megan the confidence she needed in that situation.

Teachers not only provide support to children but to parents as well. Working mothers often feel out of touch with the daily school life of their children. The mothers interviewed did not have time to be very involved in the classroom and rarely picked the children up from school. The working mothers relied on the teachers and principals to be the mothers' "eyes and ears" during the school day.

In the days before email, Kristine remembers a principal who was "legendary" about reaching out to parents about issues small and large with their children. Kristine was comforted that someone was looking out for her daughter when she could not be there.

Today it is easier than ever for working mothers to connect with their children's teachers. I am assured by my step-daughter Caroline, a sixth-grade teacher, that teachers appreciate focused communications with and feedback from parents. Working mothers should not forget to thank these teachers for all they are doing for their children. While the children remember the good teachers many years later, it is unlikely they express their appreciation while they are in the class. That is for the parents to do, because working parents need these teachers to look out for their children.

Others Can Reach Children When Parents Cannot

Especially during adolescence, children often find role models outside of their home. Gina remembers her son Angus as being extremely resourceful as a child. However, he attended several high schools where his independent thinking and lack of respect for rules were not fully appreciated. Angus finally ended up connecting with his high school philosophy teacher, Brother Mark, who was happy to engage Angus in discussions on life. Gina remembers that Brother Mark told her son many of the same things his parents were telling him but, she says, "When I spoke to him I think he just heard static. Somehow the words of Brother Mark came through."

Nicole L remembers a teacher who gained the respect of her students and made their lives easier during those difficult adolescent years. "I had an English teacher junior and senior years who had a class of fourteen students where you had to apply to be accepted. It was a two-year course. My two best friends were in the class with me. It was great to have a teacher who supported me and my friends and made everyone feel included during that 'where do I belong?' phase in high school."

Teachers can deliver tough messages if they think someone is not behaving well, and the students are more likely to listen to the teacher than a parent. Drew said, "I was a pain in the butt and the class clown—the new kid trying to make friends. My advisor was a positive influence in my life, like a mom. She was distinguished, well spoken, and a great teacher. Later in high school when I was rebelling and drinking, I started thinking I was really cool and skipped class and was listening to rap music. She pulled me aside and said that while she liked me, there was a 'new me' that crept in once in a while and she did not think that new person was really me. It was my wake-up call and resonated with me."

These teachers all stepped in to offer unsolicited advice, which was not part of their job description but made an impact on their students. Working mothers may sometimes feel jealous that teachers spend so much time with their children and have such an impact—but mothers should not worry. Children know who their parents are, and if teachers can provide insights and strong role models, they only support the parenting done at home.

Grandparents Make Children Feel Loved

Grandparents have always played a unique role in a child's life. They can provide another source of love and attention without being the disciplinarian. Children in the survey mentioned grandmothers more often than grandfathers. The grown children surveyed were asked, "Were there adults other than your parents who had a significant positive influence on you? If so, how did they impact you?" The choices below were for "Grandmother."

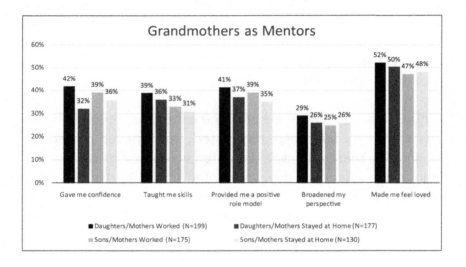

Grandmothers make children feel loved, give them confidence, and provide positive role models, according to the survey.

More children of working mothers mentioned their grandparents than the children of stay-at-home mothers. Perhaps these children appreciated the extra time the grandparents had to offer, or it could be these grandparents stepped in to help more while the parents were at work.

When Gay started her advertising company, her mother moved to Austin to be near Gay and her family. Gay says this arrangement was the "secret" to her being able to focus on growing her business. "My mother was not childcare, but she was the best grandmother. She worked at the church pre-school and took Rebecca back and forth with her. She drove the kids places. If the laundry piled up, she did it. She was really the rock that held everything down. She was a huge part of my success."

Rebecca talked about her grandmother as having a significant impact on her life. Although Rebecca's grandmother did not live in the same house, Rebecca remembers "I grew up with her being around all the time. She helped raise me. She took me to classes and activities and was always there. She was a wonderful part of my childhood."

Rebecca's grandmother had bone cancer as a teenager and her right arm had been amputated, but it never slowed her down. She married, had a daughter, was a first grade teacher, and started her own daycare center when her daughter was young. She became a widow at a young age but continued to support her family. She was a great role model for both Gay and Rebecca.

Rebecca remembers her grandmother as "extremely independent. She was really kind and loved people, but she instilled in me that you need to be independent and be strong. Everyone loved her."

Gay agrees that her mother was a wonderful influence on the children, including her husband's two sons from a prior marriage. "Mom was a great mentor to all of the kids. She taught them values. She corrected them in polite ways. A huge reason they turned out the way they did is that she had an ability and natural skills in coaching children."

Boys appreciate their grandparents too. Nick and Zach were lucky that their father's parents lived around the corner and they could walk to their grandparents' house. Zach and Nick both mentioned their grandfather, who practiced medicine until he was eighty-four, as a role model and mentor.

Zach said, "I have very fond memories of my grandfather. He was always upbeat, positive, and energized. It rubbed off on me. He also had a very strong character. He was non-judgmental and treated everyone as an equal. He always cared about what I had to say, even as a child. It is really powerful to have someone who connects with you like that one on one. I aspire to be like him."

Nick said, "Dad's dad was the patriarch of the family. He was a great storyteller, and my brother and I idolized him. He was a big figure in our lives. The people who knew him felt they lived a happier life by having known him."

Grandparents do not have to be doctors or entrepreneurs to be a special force in their grandchildren's lives. Beth remembers her grandmother as a mentor. "My Nana was a strong personality. She was not a powerhouse in the terms of a job, but she was strong and I learned a lot from her. She was very caring and you never questioned where you stood with her. She was so proud of her grandchildren. She would carry a picture book in her pocketbook and show it to anyone. She told people how smart and beautiful her grandchildren were. I learned a lot from her about how to positively interact with people."

Working mothers' first reaction may be to look to grandparents for childcare, but that is not the norm. According to AARP, the average age when someone becomes a grandparent is forty-seven, and most people are still working at that age. AARP reports only 16 percent of grandparents provide regular childcare ("New AARP Study"). Having grandparents in their lives, and not just as babysitters, is beneficial for children. Grandparents have an impact and special bond.

Working mothers should make time for children to see their grandparents, even if it means traveling to see them. Sometimes working mothers resent using any of their limited weekend time with their children to be with other relatives, especially if the grandparents or others do not share the parents' childrearing guidelines. Relax. It is okay if the children have a little too much sugar, stay up too late, or watch too much TV on occasion. The children will get the benefit of their grandparents' unconditional love, and the working parents might get a little time to themselves.

Family and Friends Can Provide Support

Other family members and family friends were also mentioned in the survey and interviews as having a positive influence. Peter D remembers being very difficult when he was an adolescent. "I did not like whatever my mother said. I was hard set on being a thorn in her side. I didn't like school that much and objected to taking subjects I didn't like."

Peter was able to find someone else to talk to during these years. "My godmother, Aunt Carol, had a profound impact on me. She was a former high school teacher, and she felt so real. I felt so confident speaking to her and knew she would give me a straightforward answer."

When Justin was five years old, his family moved to a house with three acres and a barn, and he spent as much time as possible outside. Justin did not like attending school and since he was not a conforming student, his mother started home schooling in fourth grade. He was attracted to horses and said, "Every horse is different. I liked working with them."

Justin spent a lot of time on a farm owned by family friends, Mel and Bruce, who he describes as "second parents." Bruce taught Justin how to train cutting horses—which became Justin's career for a while. "Cutting was really fun. You meet all kinds of people in the spectrum of the equine world. The people, shows, and circuit were great." What Justin remembers most about that time, however, was Bruce. "Bruce is a very hard working man. He built up his family farm and he taught me my work ethic. He taught me how to go from being a kid to a young man to a man."

Susan C, Justin's mother, was grateful for the role model Bruce provided. Susan and her husband divorced when Justin was ten years old and Justin's father moved about an hour away. Having Bruce nearby provided another adult to watch out for Justin. Susan said, "It was fascinating to watch Bruce mentor Justin. Bruce took him to board of director meetings where he met trainers and owners. He got the kind of mentoring people often talk about."

Working mothers appreciated the mentoring that family and friends provided to their children. Rather than seeing these other adults as a threat, the working mothers viewed these people in the broader context of mentoring that they saw daily in the workplace. The working mothers understood that their children welcomed advice from other adults, and the mothers appreciated the perspective these adults offered.

Working mothers can embrace other mentors for their children, whether they are teachers, grandparents, or family friends. These other adults can shape children into healthy, resilient people. You cannot, and should not, try to do it all yourself. It can be a relief to know you are not raising your children alone, and it is good that children understand they have many people who care about them and guide them. It does indeed take a village.

Chapter 10

Sports: My Mother Taught Me Sports Aren't Just for Athletes

During the early years, sports take place in someone's backyard or driveway. Playing with children outdoors— or having them play with friends—is an easy way for busy working parents to let their children have fun without too much advance planning. Monique says, "We played T-ball in the yard. My mom would help me line up the ball on the T. She and Dad would run around with us and sometimes pretend to strike out."

For some children, sports were an outlet for their energy and a major focus when they were young. Ben loved to play any type of sports. "My house was where we played basketball, football, everything. I was always out in the driveway doing something." Zach remembers, "When I was younger, I was very focused on sports and that's all I wanted to talk about."

Even parents who were not athletes themselves realized that playing a sport offers many benefits and would allow a child to gain physical confidence. Deborah did not come from a sports-minded family, but when she was in seventh grade, her science teacher and basketball coach "helped me play basketball even though I am short. He was encouraging and supportive."

Sports Provide Structure for Children and Parents

Working mothers found athletic programs a safe place for their children to spend after-school hours, especially in the middle school years when childcare is not an easy sell to adolescents. There were some variations between the genders so the numbers below are broken down that way. Since other after-school activities provided the same structured environment as sports, a chart on those participation rates is provided as well. The overall question was, "Please evaluate your general school experience at each school level through high school." And the choices were "Participated in athletics" for the first chart and "Participated in other school activities" for the second chart.

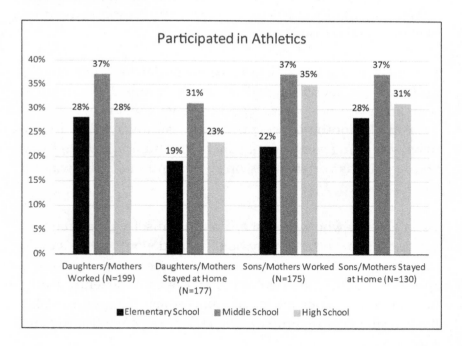

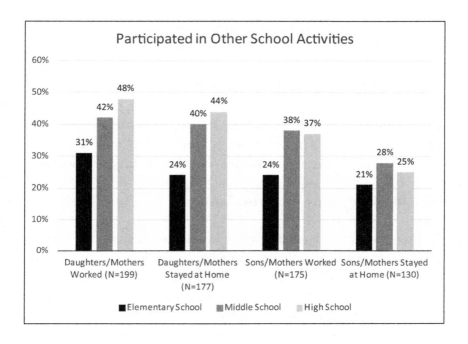

The charts above show that both daughters and sons of working mothers participated in sports and after-school activities at high rates during all levels of school, more than children of stay-at-home mothers, with the exception of sons of working mothers who reported lower levels of sports in elementary school than sons of mothers who stayed at home. As seen in the interviews, working mothers saw value in sports and used these and other after-school activities to keep their children occupied while the parents worked. One mother, Maryalice, spoke for many when she said, "I kept my daughters busy. Sports, activities, summer camps. I thought that was better than being at home with a babysitter."

The predictability of sports schedules was a tremendous benefit for working mothers, allowing them to plan ahead. Kristine says, "I knew that every Wednesday and Saturday my children would have games. I could block it off on my calendar and be there. I might not have been able to be there for practice, but I made as many games as I could. It was a very visible way of showing support for my children."

Karen loved seeing her daughter Beth play softball and become the captain of both her field hockey and ice hockey teams. Karen loved attending both her children's sporting events and made their games a priority on her calendar. "I was there to be supportive. I was an enthusiastic cheerleader on the sidelines."

Sports Offer Many Ways to Connect

Children's sports were a way for working mothers to connect to their community. When children are young, many towns have programs that are an introduction to a sport, and these relaxed sessions provide a place for parents to meet casually while rooting for their children. This setting can be an excellent way to meet other parents with children around the same age. Working mothers can meet both mothers who are staying at home and other working mothers, and they can all find common interests. Mothers talk about "bonding" with other mothers on the sidelines, and then staying in touch about upcoming signups or other town events.

Sports games can also be a good way for grandparents to connect with the family, and as we saw previously, grandparents are very important in their grandchildren's lives. Kristine says, "My children's sports were a huge part of our family life and we still talk about it. My parents came to games as often as they could. It was a nice family thing to do. It was an easy way for them to participate in my children's lives."

Watching from the sidelines, mothers could casually see who their children really were hanging out with. Another benefit mentioned by the working mothers interviewed was driving children home from the games with their teammates.

Kristine says, "It was great to have them in the car and listen to what was really going on. The best times were when they were in the back seat with their buddies, talking, and they would forget I was even there."

Coaches Can Be Another Role Model

Coaches can be a positive influence on children, and many of the lessons learned are not just about sports. Catherine says, "My cross country coach was inspiring. He taught me to be the best you can be." Jean also remembers her track coach. "Of course he taught me running skills, but he also taught me life skills."

Children of working mothers especially found that coaches taught them skills, gave them confidence, and provided positive role models. The question was, "Were there adults other than your parents who had a significant positive influence on you? If so, how did they impact you?" The choices below were for "Athletic coach."

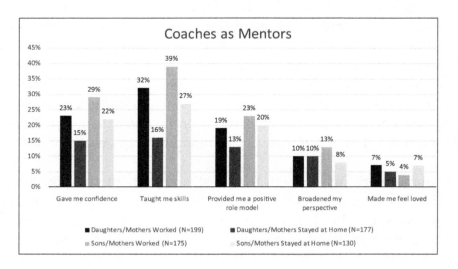

Children sometimes take advice from a coach that they may not always take to heart in the same way when it comes from a parent. A coach can be a great asset to a child's self-esteem and encourage him or her to work hard. Some coaches have an ongoing impact.

Peter D played hockey. He said, "I had such a good experience that I am still active as a player and have become a coach after work. Coaching has been a tremendous part of my life. It allows me to combine the leadership styles of people I worked with over the years. I am still young enough to know what teenagers want from a coach."

Toni is glad her son David had the experience of playing football in college. "David's football coach at Amherst was a legend. It was all about teamwork and sportsmanship. He told the players they were there to go to school, not just play sports." The right kind of coaches have a lasting influence.

Judy was impressed with the female coach of the men's crew team where Judy's daughter Jen was the coxswain. "At the time it was unusual for a woman to be coaching a men's crew team. She taught my daughter what true leadership is. She told Jen, 'You have to understand people and live the life of the people you are trying to lead so when you ask them to jump, they will jump.' Jen did all of the running and calisthenics the boys did. The coach was very influential and a great advisor."

Some working mothers felt so strongly about the positive impact of sports on their children that they found time to become coaches themselves. When Sylvia moved to Boston, she wanted to get involved in her children's school but thought the guys at the office would not think very highly of her being a class mom. However, she observed that many of the men were coaches for their kids' teams.

Even though Sylvia had not coached before, she took advantage of town-sponsored classes to become a coach. Sylvia coached her daughter Lauren's soccer team all the way through high school and son Evan's team when he was young. As an added benefit, many parents told her they were happy the children had a female coach and said she was a great role model. Sylvia was able to spend quality time with her children, give back to her community, and also be accepted at work by her sports-oriented colleagues.

It is a fact that many executives coach their children's teams. They may not be the head coach and work demands may prevent them from getting to all of the practices, but they stay involved with their children's lives through coaching. Working mothers, no matter how demanding their jobs might be, should consider this as well.

Lessons from Sports Translate Well to Life

The working mothers interviewed knew sports taught their children a number of lessons on teamwork, leadership, and strategy that would be useful later in life and in business.

Karen was an athlete herself. She says, "In an individual sport, you learn how to be super competitive for yourself—to push yourself to be the best you can be. Those are good skills to learn, but I encouraged my children to go into team sports as well. In team sports, the goal is for the team to win, so you need to optimize the group performance. Team play is a critical success factor in business because you need to work collaboratively with others." Karen, a former point guard, used an analogy to make her argument. "It is like basketball where you can't hog the ball. If you do, you might get more shots yourself, but the team will lose. You need to pass the ball, leverage the skills of your teammates."

Marcia said in her family the children were not able to quit a sport once they started the season. Marcia and her husband told the children, "If you start something, you have to finish it, you can't walk away. There were times the kids would have left a team or dropped an activity, but in our family we have a saying—finish well."

Anne is not sure whether it was her crew coaches or her team members who taught her the most, but believes being part of a crew team changed her life. "It was four years where someone owned my life. It was both the coaches and crew. It taught me teamwork, reliability, and consistency, listening to criticism, being able to handle the truth, working with it and not getting defensive. When you lose, work harder and don't give up. We did it through crew. It was so intertwined. One thing I have done well is I handle failure well. I bounce well."

Maryalice coached basketball and felt her daughters learned many positive lessons from sports. "Sports is real to kids. They learn that you have to work hard to win. They learn how to balance practice and games with schoolwork. It is tough to fail and lose in front of your friends, but they learn how to lose with dignity. Sports builds confidence and poise. You learn how to work as a team. When I coached, we had a girl with special needs and I gave her equal playing time. The girls on the team learned to respect her." Sports teach children about diversity, the importance of inclusion, and working together as a team. These lessons will serve them well in school, business, and other areas of life for years to come.

Several mothers mentioned that their children learned to think strategically by playing sports. Sylvia says of the soccer coach who coached her son, "He was a 'head game' person and got Evan to think strategically. He would tell Evan to anticipate and go where the ball should be."

Kristine went even further. "My son learned a lot of strategy playing soccer. He would look at where the players would line up. Think about where the ball is going. He was always good at math but soccer has an almost chess-like feature—you need to think about what is coming many moves ahead. Ask yourself what is going to happen and where you need to position yourself. Leverage your team and communicate with them where they need to be." Kristine believes her son has taken this skill with him into the business world. "He is always thinking strategically and wondering what will impact his business next year."

There Are Many Ways to Engage for a Win

Not every mother has the time or money to enroll her children in organized sports, but you can find ways to get your children engaged. Just like at work, we can outsource.

Janet lived in New York, and since she was a single parent, money was tight in their household. Her son Kevin went on weekend get-aways with friends who they taught him athletic activities like ocean surfing and skateboarding. Janet says she and Kevin's father weren't athletic and couldn't teach him those things, so she thought it was great that Kevin was exposed to these activities.

My side of the family is not in the least bit athletic. My children would say I "failed" at exposing them to sports in general, but they did manage to become excellent skiers. When we moved to Boston, my daughter was nine and my son was five. That first winter we were invited to go away for a ski weekend. Undeterred by my complete lack of knowledge, we all went to a ski store, bought the appropriate clothes, and rented equipment. I knew sports were not my list of core competencies, so I booked lessons for all of us. Even now I am most comfortable on easy slopes, but my children can ski down any slope they encounter. We still do family ski vacations—and meet up at the end of the afternoon after we have our separate skiing experiences.

Even if you were not an athlete yourself or your child is not especially talented, the lessons learned in sports are important, and it is beneficial to expose children to various sports for all of the lessons they need to be successful in life, such as teamwork, discipline, persistence, experiencing failure, leadership, and strategic thinking.

The lessons described here about sports can also be applied to other activities like dance, riding, Scouts, and music. Working hard to be your best individually and as part of a team, be it a sports team or a choir, takes dedication and hard work. Being involved and learning something new builds a child's confidence and gives him or her opportunities for new friendships and new mentors.

For working mothers, athletics and extracurricular activities can provide another way to be a part of children's lives. Because games and events are scheduled well in advance, working mothers can block the dates out on their calendars so they can attend. Working mothers should also consider coaching or being the den mother. Don't leave all the fun to the fathers.

Athletic and other activities provide an easy way for you to regularly interact with your children, other mothers, and feel a part of the community. It is the ultimate "win."

Chapter 11

Life Skills: My Mother Taught Me to Deal with People and Problems

Knowing how to deal with people is crucial throughout life. Many of the children surveyed used their mothers to help them with general people skills. Mothers also knew that as their children grew, mothers could not control the environment, so they needed to give their children the skills necessary to deal with difficult situations.

The survey questions that provide the data for the charts in this chapter were asked in the context of jobs, which will be covered in the next chapter, but it was clear in the interviews that many lessons were taught by mothers from the time the children were born; they did not just start when the children were looking for employment.

Parents Are the First Teachers

Grown children remember their parents teaching them how to behave and what was acceptable in their homes and in society. Working mothers, whose young children spend much of their waking hours being cared for by others, have to be very deliberate in teaching their children how to conduct themselves. Mothers can be exhausted by the time they get home at night, and it is easy to let things slide, but that is not good for the children in the long run. As one of my friends says, "Well behaved children are welcome anywhere."

My father used to tell a story of when he first became a parent. He sought the advice of another man he respected and admired who had raised three daughters. He asked the man, "What is the secret?" The older man said, "Lots of love and lots of discipline."

I have always remembered that story. There was a lot of love when I was raising my children, but there were also a lot of rules and expected behaviors. Love and discipline are quite compatible. When my son was around two, I was afraid he would think his name was, "No, Paul." He, of course, does not remember this.

Children appreciate their upbringing when they are adults. Some people-skill behavior is specifically taught, but much of it is just absorbed by children watching their parents. Rick, now a parent himself, says, "My approach to discipline is identical to my parents. When we are at a restaurant it is really important for the kids to be well behaved, be polite, and not be too loud. To this day people remark about my manners. I don't remember my parents pushing it into me, but it permeated everything."

As children got older, parents focused on the important lessons of how to treat other people. Daniel remembers his mother telling him "The Golden Rule: treat others the way you wanted to be treated yourself." Chris says, "My mother taught me to treat people decently. Be honest. Be a good person." Ben said something very similar. "Mom taught me kindness, compassion, looking out for other people, being a good person, and being genuine."

The question that provided the data for the chart below was, "Have you found your mother helpful with job searches or your work experience at any point in your career?" The specific choice was "People skills" and the percentages are for "very helpful."

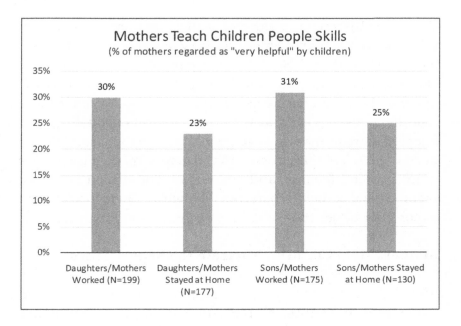

David B and Jeffrey both have tremendous admiration for their mother and the lessons she taught them. David recounted "She taught me to me a good person." Jeffrey says, "She taught me empathy. She did not preach it to us, just demonstrated it on a daily basis."

Many mothers and children spoke of the roles mothers played in helping children figure out how to develop true friendships with others. Danielle's mother taught her that having a strong group of friends was important to staying happy. She recalls her mother saying, "Make sure you preserve your relationships—partner, family, and friends." Her brother Josh also commented on his mother's work friendships. "I admire how my mother developed strong and special relationships with her co-workers. I did not realize until I was older that this was unusual."

Several of the grown children felt their mothers were ethical role models. Zach says, "Mom is a very moral person. She says, 'Do the right thing.' Now this is a part of me. I live by that. Dad supported this, but Mom really drove the point across." Drew had similar comments about his parents. "Mom is more morally focused. Dad and I can be cold and calculating. She injected more humanity. I can push things to the side if I do not need them to get things done. Her presence made me consider other people's feelings and emotions." These men were not being critical of their fathers, but felt their mothers forced them to consider issues they might not recognize on their own.

Mothers Help Children Navigate the School Years

Mothers taught more specific lessons as children grew and sometimes encountered bullying or cliques. Remember from an earlier chapter that many children felt left out, and approximately one in four said they were bullied during school years. It was up to the parents and the other adults in their lives to help children manage problematic situations and to give them support and the skills to manage these difficult years. While this is a challenge for all parents, it was especially hard for working mothers who were away from home for longer hours. A number of mothers mentioned that since they were not at home when their children got out of school, they did not always know what they had missed. As Marcia said, "As a working mom, you don't know what accumulates during the day, you only get a certain view."

The question that provided the data for the chart below was, "Have you found your mother helpful with job searches or your work experience at any point in your career?" The specific choice was "Taught me to be resilient, how to rebound from setbacks" and the percentages are for "very helpful."

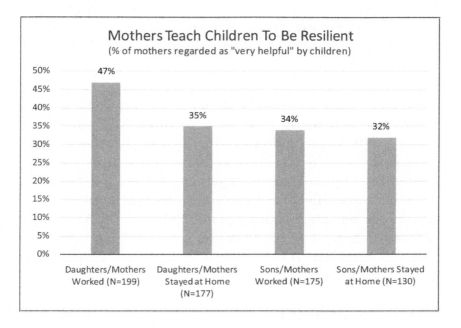

Mothers Teach Children To Be Resilient
(% of mothers regarded as "very helpful" by children)

Lisa B remembers talking to her children about resiliency "I would tell my daughter that you don't always need to follow the crowd. She struggled and wanted to be one of the 'cool kids,' but I told my kids they needed to go back to who they were." She told her children, "Have a plan. Don't wait for it to happen to you (whatever 'it' is). Be clear about what you want and why you want it. Don't just follow the flow. This helped our daughter in particular with girl dynamics in those tough sixth through ninth grade years. We told her it was okay to feel isolated and alone because being a part of 'them' would cause 'you' to compromise yourself. Only you can make yourself feel bad."

Maryalice taught her daughters about resiliency by telling stories of her own difficulties at work and setting an example of overcoming obstacles. "I talked to them about difficult bosses, having to lay people off, and how hard it was when I changed jobs. Maybe the best lesson was when they saw me go through a divorce, move, and start a new life in another city. One of my daughters told me she was so proud of me and who I had become."

Nancy felt very deeply about her daughter Nicole being strong enough to find her way through difficult times. Nancy had been widowed during her first marriage, long before her daughter was born, but it impacted her parenting. "I taught her independence. I wanted her to be able to handle anything that comes her way. I told her she needed to be self-resourceful and self-reliant. At the age of twenty-five, I had my legs knocked out from under me and I wanted her to be resilient. You never know what is going to happen."

These working mothers knew bad things could happen in life. They knew they could not always protect their children, so they wanted to give them the skills to solve the problems on their own. Laura H said, "We taught them to figure things out for themselves. We weren't particularly protective. They had a lot of independence. We believed the most important thing was to teach kids confidence, competence in life things, and independence. For example, if they asked, 'Can I have an egg?' we'd say 'Yes, I'll show you how to make it.'"

The question that provided the data for the chart below was, "Have you found your mother helpful with job searches or your work experience at any point in your career?" The specific choice was "Taught me to be independent" and the percentages are for "very helpful."

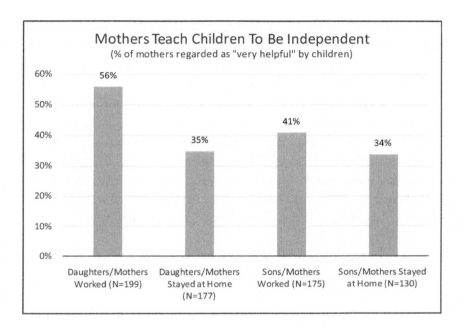

One response that stands out is that **56 percent of daughters** of working mothers say their mother was very helpful in teaching them to be independent. Perhaps working mothers understood the challenges their daughters would face in the workplace and wanted them to be prepared.

Independent children are a mixed blessing. A friend of mine once said, "The good news is we taught our children to be independent. The bad news is we taught our children to be independent." Independent children think for themselves, and the decisions they come to are not always the ones mothers want, especially when they are teenagers. However, we need to encourage children to handle situations on their own, no matter how much we may want to step in. Tears or "everyone is doing it" never convinced me I was wrong, but a good logical argument always did. Be prepared to change your mind. Your children may be smarter than you expect them to be at a young age.

Most of the mothers interviewed talked about teaching children to be independent, but one mother said she tried to solve everything for her son. Now both she and her son agree in retrospect it did not help him. The son felt his mother was always stepping in to try to solve his problems for him. The mother only had one child, and she poured all of her energy into him. This man, when asked what his parents should have done less of, says, "Less helicoptering. They wanted to make sure everything was always good. Sunshine and rainbows. Life is not always like that, and it was a harsh awakening when I went to college and was on my own."

His mother agrees with his assessment that she missed an opportunity to teach him more life skills. In a separate interview, she said, "I wish I had spent more time early on focused on accountability. I wish I had given him more structure about making decisions. I wish I had done less of solving his problems for him. I was a helicopter parent. I would go into the 'We'll solve it mode' and give him the answer."

Adolescence is Difficult for Children and Parents

Parents know from experience that their children will survive adolescence, but this does not make the process any easier for the parents or the children. My mother used to say, "Little kids, little money, little problems. Big kids, big money, big problems." Adolescence can have some big problems, and as a mother, it is your job to get your children through these years, even if you just wish you could transport them to the other side.

Working mothers can find the teenage years especially exhausting. Just when things settle down, childcare issues are solved, and your child is settled into school, suddenly a teenager takes residence in your house. Overnight you can go from worrying about grades to wondering if your child will ever graduate from high school. Your lovely child suddenly rejects you and many of the things you have taught him or her. You go from being a source of knowledge to being "stupid." For some working mothers, this is a time they consider quitting their jobs, but staying at home will not make adolescence any easier.

Our job as mothers is to build the confidence children will need as they go out in the adult world. When teenagers are at home, it may not seem to mothers as if they are making any progress, but the grown children give their mothers a lot of credit for helping them learn to believe in themselves.

Sarah D said, "My mom believes in me 110 percent. She believes in me even when I don't believe in myself. She taught me to be comfortable with who I am. To be confident."

The question that provided the data for the chart below was, "Have you found your mother helpful with job searches or your work experience at any point in your career?" The specific choice was "Taught me to have confidence in myself" and the percentages are for "very helpful."

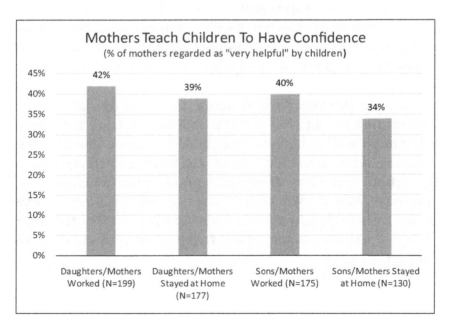

Nancy remembers, "I wish I had had a better understanding of the different stages a child goes through, especially during adolescence. There was a period my daughter got tattoos and pierced her nose. In my world, piercings and tattoos are a big deal. I wanted to know 'What happened to my little girl?' Now she is the most giving, caring, generous person in the world, but at the time she was flexing her independence."

Susannah echoed the feelings of many of the children when she said, "I didn't have the best time in middle and high school. It seemed they were run by people who all liked each other but not me. I felt like everyone got a rule book and I didn't." As a mother, your heart goes out when a child struggles, but mothers can't make these adolescent years any shorter if they stay home, so don't succumb to guilt as a working mother.

The teen years are a strain on most parent-child relationships. One young woman remembers, "Mom and I had many years when we did not get along. Middle school and high school were very rough with constant fighting and screaming. I was very verbal." Interestingly, her mother never mentioned their fighting. Maybe her mother realized it is normal for daughters to reject their mothers during adolescence; she knew her daughter was just trying to sort out who she was.

These are the years when being a "sounding board" can sometimes be painful for the mother. A friend of mine recounted a time her teenage daughter drove her to tears. She asked her daughter, "Anna, just what is it that you don't like about me?" Her daughter replied, "How much time do you have, Mom?" Working mothers need to remember this is not personal—although it feels very personal at the time. You are just the person who is there when your child needs to vent.

As children test limits, you need to be patient and remember the skills you learn at work about dealing with difficult situations. One night, in the days before cell phones, my daughter came home much later than expected. I had been worried and then became angry, but I knew it was never a good idea to have a serious conversation when I was upset. I told her I was too angry to talk to her that night and we would discuss her actions in the morning. She told me later that nothing I had ever said had scared her as much. And we did talk in the morning when I was more rational.

The adolescent years can be hard on working mothers (all mothers). By this age, children have figured out that words can hurt, and children can attack a working mother's guilt of not being at home all the time. Don't think staying at home will bring back your angelic child—it won't. Most children are difficult during adolescence. As a parent you just need to remember this is the time your children need you to be firm. I always said to my children I would give them some room to navigate, but I would not let them run off the road. Don't worry. Your children will come back to you. By the time they get out of their teens, you will suddenly get very smart again.

Continue to talk to your children and keep the lines of communication open during these tough years, even if you think they are not listening. Peter E recommends, "Treat your kids like adults and have honest conversations with them. Tell them to be conscious of what they are doing. My parents used to say, 'Use your head and understand the consequences of your actions.'" Peter felt this helped him and his siblings get through adolescence.

Parents Help Children Connect to Their Community

Especially during the teenage years, parents strived to get their children to look outside of their own world. Susan D's husband "got the kids involved in church and he was very dedicated to that. As we became more affluent, we saw that other kids tended to focus on clothes and other things that were not important. Being involved with the church helped our children be well grounded and have good values."

Pattie said, "As a family we were always very active in non-profit work and doing things beyond our own home. Our son was raised in a religious environment, but it was faith in action. We wanted to go make a difference in the world."

Very few of us take parenting classes, so most mothers have to figure out on their own how to raise well-behaved and kind children. Many of the working mothers described themselves as the disciplinarian in the family. In fact, because they worked and their hours with their children were limited, it was more important than ever to set rules and encourage good behavior. Raising children to have people skills will serve them their whole life. As shown in the survey and the interviews, children relied on their mothers to be their teacher for these important skills. The challenge of these years is worth it; it pays lifelong dividends.

Chapter 12

Careers: My Mother Taught Me How to Get a Job

All parents want their children to have a job they enjoy which supports their lifestyle. In today's economy, it is the rare parent who can actually get a position for a child, but parents can prepare their children for employment. In the survey, working mothers had a big edge in providing advice to their children. The overall question was, "Have you found your mother helpful with job searches or your work experience at any point in your career?" The option below was for "Career discussions."

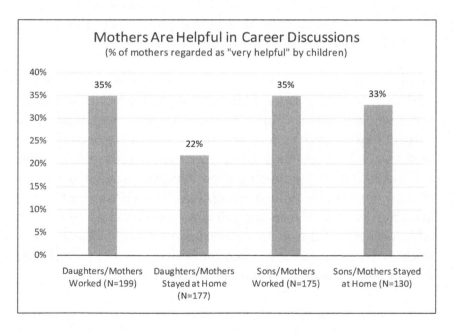

The survey shows that all mothers helped their children, but the advice provided by working mothers on career discussions was deemed "very helpful" by more children. Both daughters and sons of working mothers said they received more useful advice from their mothers than their fathers.

Career Discussions Start Early

Working mothers assumed their children would also work and expressed this to their children during the years they were growing up. Danielle says, "My mom is a very feminist woman. She liked to work, and it was a financial necessity. Part of her identity was her work and she talked about it with her kids. As a woman, I was expected to grow up and have a career."

Maggie says her mother "taught us business terms at breakfast." For many mothers, the conversations first started around what the child was good at, what they liked to do, and what courses in college they should be taking that would help them get a good job.

I had very specific conversations with my children about grades and college. They were both interested in many subjects, but I advised them to take rigorous courses and major in a subject like math or economics that would be respected in the business world, which is where my career took place. I also encouraged them to keep up their grades. I knew from years of interviewing on college campuses that GPAs matter and are often used as a screening device to even get an interview. Although my children took courses in many subjects, they both majored in business economics in college, which they used as springboards to completely different careers.

Zach says, "Both of my parents are very goal oriented. I was raised to think about performance and grades. They never pressured me, but there was pressure because it was implicit in how you were evaluated. Be successful at what you do."

Working mothers get very high marks from the children interviewed for helping them analyze what they wanted to do. Jamie says of his mother, "She helped me figure out which companies were good companies. She helped me understand what the good positions were." Daniel has a similar comment about his mother. "In my job search, I had no idea what I wanted to do but Mom helped me figure it out. Other friends had to figure this out on their own."

Even if mothers had different interests than their children, they supported their children in their choices. Caitlyn, whose mother Joanie was in finance, is studying for a PhD in psychology. Caitlyn says of her mother, "What I do freaks her out. It is so different from what she does. My job is the last thing she'd want to do, and her job is the last thing I'd want to do. However, she's always been extremely supportive of me. I've wanted to be a child psychologist since high school. She never tried to steer me into something she was familiar with. All three of the daughters in our family do different things." Mothers don't need to be in the same field to provide advice and support.

For some mothers, focusing their children early on a career was a way to build in options. Maryalice says, "I told them they were getting the gift of education. I was always messaging expectations. I did not want them to be stuck in a marriage or job they did not like. I wanted them to have choices."

Some of the best advice parents provided was to steer children away from a career mistake. Matt says, "My parents forced the kids to think of career options before making choices. For example, I wanted to be a cook but my parents said I had to go to college first. I could always go to a culinary school later. They said, 'The best thing in life is having options.'" Matt did go to college and did not become a cook.

When Josh graduated from college, he was considering starting a composting operation in Boston, but his parents were concerned about the prospect of its success. They acted as a sounding board. He called it "a mix of concern and support." In the end, he decided not to start the business. Instead, he moved to New York where he started a food business. It was not that his parents objected to his entrepreneurial inclination, but they questioned his business model and helped him avoid what they thought would be an early failure.

Looking For a Job

What did the grown children look for in a job? For most people, a number of factors are considered when deciding on a job. The table below indicates the weighted average rankings.

Ranking	Daughters/ Mothers Worked (N=199)	Daughters/ Mothers Stayed Home (N=177)	Sons/Mothers Worked (N=175)	Sons/Mothers Stayed Home (N=130)
1	Schedule flexibility	Schedule flexibility	Compensation	Compensation
2	Compensation	Compensation	Health care benefits	Opportunities for career growth
3	Opportunities for career growth	Health care benefits	Opportunities for career growth	Schedule flexibility
4	Health care benefits	Opportunities for career growth	Schedule flexibility	Health care benefits
5	Intellectually stimulating work	Intellectually stimulating work	Intellectually stimulating work	Liking the people you work with
6	Paid time off	Paid time off	Paid time off (tie)	Intellectually stimulating work
7	Liking the people you work with	Liking the people you work with	Liking the people you work with (tie)	Paid time off
8	Retirement benefits	Retirement benefits	Retirement benefits	Retirement benefits
9	Parental leave	Parental leave	Parental leave	Parental leave

Money is at the top of the sons' wish lists and is ranked second by the daughters, but what is most striking are the other criteria. The other major job attribute mentioned was schedule flexibility (time off for appointments, family time, etc.). The grown children interviewed made it clear their generation was different from their parents; they would not let work dominate their lives. (More on this in the chapter on success.) It may be that the daughters mentioned flexibility as their number one attribute because they had seen their mothers take on a disproportionate share of the household duties.

The top four job criteria were the same for sons and daughters of both working and stay-at-home mothers, even if the ranking was slightly different:

- Compensation
- Schedule flexibility (time off for appointments, family time, etc.)
- Opportunities for career growth
- Health care benefits

Compensation, schedule flexibility, and opportunities for career growth are not surprising, but health care benefits might not have been at the top of a list a generation ago. The recent national debate on health care most likely raised the issue on people's minds as the costs have been discussed.

Prepare Well for Interviews

Once children were actually in the job market, working mothers had very specific advice about how to look, act, and speak. They also helped edit and proof résumés. Even though they might have very different interests than their children, they knew there were commonalities in a job search.

Susannah says, "My mother has always been there with advice on how to communicate, what to wear, and what questions to ask." Peter D agreed. "Both of my parents gave me advice. They were there with résumés, interviews, and career guidance. They are still there."

Nick described the assistance he got from his mother. "I knew I had to get a job and make myself marketable. Mom is excellent at this. She really understands how the system works. She is very good at the tangible aspects of finding the right job and how institutions hire."

Deborah's mother provided major assistance to her. Deborah says, "She did everything from taking me suit shopping to line-by-line editing of my résumé. The other critical component is she helped me craft my story. She elicited stories from me and helped me articulate *my* story." This was a common theme. The working mothers knew their children had to stand out in a crowded market. Catherine says her mother not only edited her résumé but talked to her "about how I should present myself."

When interviews did not go well, mothers could help prepare their children to do better next time. Monique is in the hospitality industry and her mother Susan M had a career in banking, but she could still provide some great advice. Monique said, "My mother helped me prepare for interviews and how to answer questions. Once I had a terrible interview when I was asked the question, 'Do you think the customer is always right?' and she told me next time to answer it, 'No, but we always provide the best service we can.' Now that I am interviewing people, I use that question every time. It is the best advice she ever gave me. She taught me how to handle myself and not to shy away from confrontation."

Mothers seemed to feel their daughters needed a little extra advice. Nicole says of her mother, "She taught me how to hold myself and present myself. She is a very classy person. I respect her and learned from her. She taught me how to dress and how to talk to people. She taught me how to use my intelligence, not my femininity."

Networking Is Important

Very few of the children chose the same career path as their parents, so what working mothers were able to provide were contacts and general business advice. When the children were in college, some mothers helped their children get internships by reaching out to colleagues and friends. The overall question was, "Have you found your mother helpful with job searches or your work experience at any point in your career?" The option below was for "Networking/Introductions" and the percentages were for "very helpful."

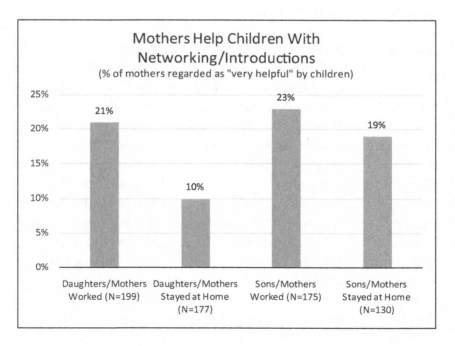

Zach says, "Mom always knows people who are willing to talk to me who have a good perspective. The experience of having access to highly successful professionals has shaped my perspective and prepared me for that culture." Lauren J also used her mother's contacts. "Because of her various connections and activities in the community, she knew a lot of people I could call and network with."

When asked whether her mother provided her with ideas or assistance when she was looking for a job, Maggie said, "Yes. I was thankful she was in business because she knew it was all about networking. My friends' parents didn't give them that advice."

Alix knew she wanted to do something meaningful, where she could give back, but was not sure how to go about the process. Her mother Kathleen helped her identify companies and got introductions through her own coworkers. Kathleen says, "This was the first time I used my contacts for a referral. Men have been doing it for years. Alix just needed the opportunity to sell herself." Alix started working as a counselor in a residential home for at-risk youth. Alix says of her mother, "She helped me find the position I never knew I wanted but changed my life." It is not the highest paying job, but Kathleen told her daughter, "Do what you are most passionate about and the money will follow."

The children interviewed from entrepreneurial families were more inclined to become entrepreneurs themselves. Maybe they were just exposed to small businesses from an earlier age. Ben says, "In our childhood, all the parents worked. Since my parents both owned their businesses, the business was a big part of our lives growing up. The lines were more blurred between home and business."

Being part of an entrepreneurial family "helped shape who I am," said Ben. "It was what we talked about at dinner. Mom would pick us up from school and talk to clients on the phone while she drove us home. We always knew what was going on." Ben went into the family advertising business and his sister Rebecca started her own clothing business.

Like most working mothers, I used my circle of friends and colleagues to help my children consider career decisions. My children trusted my opinion, but they also understood the value of getting advice from other individuals who had been successful in other professions.

Only one grown child criticized her mother for doing too much. When she was in college, her mother got her internships during two summers. The daughter never had to interview, just show up. When the daughter was looking for full-time employment, she said, "I wasn't prepared for interviews. I did not realize how judgmental the process could be. I wasn't prepared for the harsh reality of rejection. My mother always told me I could do anything." This reaffirms the statement made in the last chapter when the son said his mother trying to do everything did not help him in the long run. Helping children get a foot in the door or an interview is wonderful. Getting them a job does not build confidence or skills.

Careers Can Change

Working mothers continued to provide advice long after the first job. They knew their children would have many career moves, and they provided welcome advice along the way. The children of working mothers, especially the daughters, have found their mothers useful sounding boards. The overall question was, "Have you found your mother helpful with job searches or your work experience at any point in your career?" The option below was for "General sounding board" and the percentages were for "very helpful."

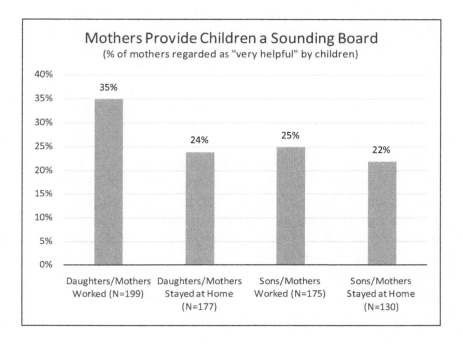

Maggie says, "Through all of my job searches and the setback of being laid off, she keeps telling me she has experienced these personally. She is more supportive now than she ever has been." Her brother Peter agrees. "There has been a shift in our relationship. My mother is much more a mentor to me now that I am married and have a career of my own, and I am very grateful. She's a great resource for career advice and gives knowledge I can utilize myself."

Deborah continued to talk to her mother as her career progressed. "She helped guide me and figure out how to find mentors, how to get people to adopt me and help me be successful."

There were times mothers could provide specific guidance. Megan wanted to be involved with the environment, but without a science background she knew this was challenging. Her mother helped her think about ways to use her business degree to achieve her goals. Megan worked in the finance department at a major university, got her master's in sustainability at employee tuition rates, and then was able to change careers and become a sustainability manager.

Sometimes it was the parents themselves who provided the role model of changing a career. When Kathleen and her husband Steve married, they had three children from previous marriages and their expenses included alimony and child support payments. Steve, a successful salesman in the construction industry, wanted to go into education but their budget did not allow for a reduction in the family income. Kathleen and Steve devised a plan for him to get his master's degree in education at night when he was in his mid-forties in order to position himself for a career move in the future.

Over time, Kathleen's income rose and the family expenses decreased as the children graduated from college. Together they decided when it was the right time for Steve to apply for teaching positions. He is now a math teacher in an urban charter school where 94 percent of the students go to college. Kathleen says, "He is the happiest I have ever seen him." Their own children love that he is now a teacher.

Kathleen says, "We talked to all the kids about this. We wanted them to know that you can change careers if you want to. You just have to plan for it and work as a team to accomplish it. We are both fulfilling our goals and dreams."

No matter how old your children are now, remember how valuable your network will be to them when they are job hunting. Working mothers continue to have mentoring relationships with their children throughout adulthood. The business skills, experience, and networks the mothers can offer their children have tremendous value. The mother-child relationship transitions easily to an adult-adult relationship. The grown children have a deeper appreciation and understanding of their multi-talented working mothers. Many become working mothers themselves.

Chapter 13

Success: My Mother Taught Me to be Successful

Every mother wants her child to be a "successful" adult, and working mothers want to know their children will turn out just as successful as those whose mothers stay at home. Well, don't worry, they do.

"Success" is subjective and personal. While to some it may mean fame or fortune, for most people it follows the first definition in the dictionary: "The achievement of something attempted." What were the grown children attempting to achieve and in their own opinion, did they succeed?

During the personal interviews, the discussion around the definition and achievement of success raised more passion than any other subject. Many of the grown children interviewed were still trying to figure out what success meant to them; they admitted the definition had changed over time. The same can be said for any of us.

The top four choices for daughters of both working and stay-at-home mothers were the same, but for the sons they were a little different.

Daughters/ Mothers Worked (N=199)	Daughters/ Mothers Stayed at Home (N=177)	Sons/Mothers Worked (N=175)	Sons/Mothers Stayed at Home (N=130)
Partner to share my life	Children	Successful career working in an organization	Successful career working in an organization
Children	Partner to share my life	Financial success	Partner
Financial success	Successful career working in an organization	Working for myself	Time to do the things I want to do
Successful career working in an organization	Financial success	Time to do the things I want to do	Financial success

How did these priorities change over time? The chart below breaks down the answers by age group.

Age 23-29 (N=324)	Age 30-36 (N=322)	Age 37-44 (N=331)
Successful career	Successful career	*Children*
Financial success	*Partner*	*Partner*
Partner	*Children*	Successful career (tied)
Time to do things	Financial success	Financial success (tied)

As the grown children got older, careers and financial success were still highly ranked, but the importance of having a partner increased. Children first appeared highly ranked when survey participants were in their thirties and by the late thirties, children topped the list, even surpassing having a partner. The responses were very similar for children of both working and stay-at-home mothers.

So how well did the grown children do in achieving their goals? It did not matter whether the mother worked or stayed at home, a significant percentage of the children were married or in committed relationships the time they reached their thirties. The chart below indicates the response to the survey question, "What is your current relationship status?" and the percentages are for the total of "Married" and "Committed relationship."

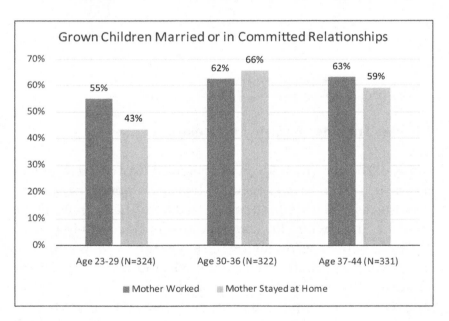

They also achieved their goals of becoming parents. Children of working mothers had children a little later than children whose mothers stayed at home, but by their late thirties, approximately 60 percent had become parents. The answers below were for the survey question, "Do you have children or plans for children in the future?" The percentages were for the answer, "Yes, I have a child/children."

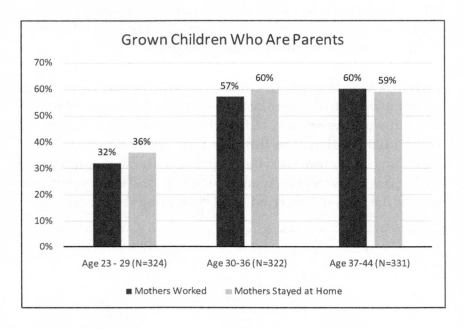

Success Includes Family and Relationships

Many of the grown children interviewed expressed family as a measure of success, especially those who were now parents themselves. Kevin defined success as "being happy most of the time, having a wife I love, and children who are doing well." Rick put being a good, loving parent at the top of his success checklist. "My greatest achievement is and will always be my children. I didn't know this until I had kids. I give them as much love and support as I can. It is more important to give them love and attention than money." He also mentioned, "It is important to have a good, solid, personal relationship. You can have all the money in the world, but if you have no one to share it with, it is meaningless."

Nicole A echoed these comments. "The average American defines success by money. I am not making much money. My company is doing well, but we are reinvesting in the business. I love living in Spain. I have a wonderful husband and children. Happiness is where you are."

Ben's definition of success has changed. "It used to be about money but I got married two years ago. Now success is about being a good husband and father and having balance in my life." Peter E is not married yet, but he agrees with Ben. "I want a family like the one I had. My parents have been married for forty-five years and they have literally grown up together. I have missed that opportunity, but it is important not to just settle. It has to be meaningful. Theirs is the type of relationship I want."

Happiness is a Measure of Success

The grown children interviewed agreed that work should be enjoyable. When asked how she defined success, Alix said, "Being happy. I have a hard time buying into the idea you need a lot of money. If you go to work and are motivated and love it and want to be there, that is good."

David believes that to be happy with life, people need to be productive, contributing members of society, whether that is working, volunteering, or raising a family. His brother Jeffrey also mentioned that his definition of success was having a feeling of accomplishment. Professionally, he wanted to be valued and rewarded for his contributions at work, not just monetarily.

Ben put family as top of his list, but he also wants fulfilling work. "If I wake up every day and do something I like and am around people I love, I would consider myself very successful."

Some of the grown children drew comparisons to their parents' generation. One son said, "I define success differently than my parents. My parents believe that your career defines who you are and if you asked who they are, they would tell you about their jobs. I love my job, but I don't define my success by the title on my business card. I need to work for money to provide for my family, but it is not related to who I am."

The grown children who were parents were pragmatic about money. Kevin said, "Money is to eat, play, and have fun. I'll have enough money when I can look to the future and see the next chapter beyond this work experience." Rick said money was on the bottom of his list, but acknowledged, "I need enough to put the kids through college and retire at some point."

Justin said, "I have seen a lot of people with a lot of money, and some are happy and some are not. If you have enough to get by, you are a success."

Following One's Passions Is Success

The upbringing working mothers provide their children does impact their choices. Josh's definition of success is working as a professional in an organization where he can help people. Both of his parents' careers have been in the non-profit world. He wants to work hard and enjoy his job, but also have time to pursue his hobbies. He says, "I am working for a non-profit and working overtly to help people. I am aware this is coming from my family background and feel it is guiding my choices. I am doing something I like and doing it well, and I still have flexibility to pursue things outside of work. Overarching all of that is the question, 'What good am I doing?' Sometimes I am overwhelmed, but I try to keep it all in perspective and my mom has really encouraged me."

Holly had a high-powered career but changed course and now introduces herself as a professional volunteer. "I started out thinking success was my career and professional accomplishments. After college I went into structural engineering, and for thirteen years worked on very high quality, large scale construction projects. When I was pregnant with my first child I wanted to change careers, so I got my MBA and went to work at a non-profit that develops affordable housing. It was very stressful, so after a while I quit, but then was depressed since my life did not fit into my definition of success, which was largely defined by my career. I finally got involved in volunteer activities and started a non-profit for the after-school programs in our town, working with incredible women to make the programs a reality. I realized my new definition of success was to take on a challenge and solve it. It is about sharing my skills. I was able to put together a team and make the program a reality."

Peter E's definition of success includes his own business. He said, "I don't equate success to just having money. Money is the easy default. For others it may be a big house and fancy car, but I want my own company and want to hire good people, grow the business, and see the company become successful. Where am I on my checklist? It would be completely empty if I do not start my own company. I am proud of what I do, but if I look back and didn't try to have my own company, I'd feel regretful."

The common theme from the interviews is everyone wants to be happy—however it is defined. As Justin said, "If you are happy in the life you have, you are a success."

Success Is a Journey

The age of the children interviewed affected their reflections. Alix agrees. "The job you have at twenty-two may not be where you want to end up, but it is a journey, discovering where you want to be."

Exactly. Rory said, "I am trying to figure out my career. What makes someone happy and a valuable member of society?" Maggie said, "Success is different for everyone. I don't know what my future definition of success will be." Her brother Peter agreed, "My definition of success fluctuates every single day, and I am trying to figure it out."

Rebecca was also questioning herself. "I am still trying to figure out what I want. I am getting there. Finding out what you are really passionate about takes a while. For a lot of people it takes a long time to get there. Success is about waking up every day and being excited about what you do. As long as you are taking steps every day to get there, it is good."

Zach was finding his own definition of both personal and professional success hard to pin down. "What I define as success has changed from year to year over the last five years. Now I am I am trying to learn what is important to me in my personal life. I want kids and a happy marriage. I can be very intense about work. I need to focus on what I will contribute to a relationship and what I aspire to. Professionally, I want to do something with my career that allows me to be creative and have autonomy. I want to have an impact early in my career. I want to do something well, that I like, that fits my personality."

Ben said, "Maybe one day you wake up and realize whether you are successful or not. I think my definition will change. I am too young to understand it all. Now I am focused on the tactical aspects of success. My aperture broadens every year."

Megan said, "I have come to realize that success is not a destination but a journey and I am very excited to be on the journey."

The Grown Children Are Doing Well

Success in life is a journey, one that we all take. When asked where they were on their own success checklist, the grown children interviewed were generally happy. The survey results indicate that whether the mother worked or not did not impact happiness. When asked how they felt about their life right now, very few were unhappy. The answers are to the survey question, "How do you feel about your life right now?"

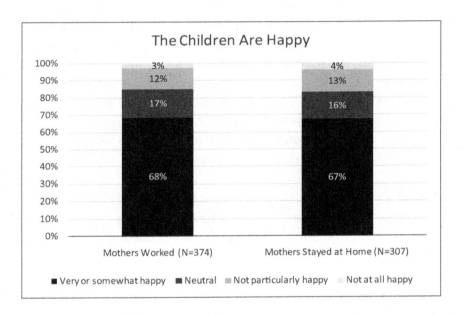

Even if they are not exactly where they want to be, the grown children interviewed are making progress. As expected, the older children were farther along on their path.

Lauren H reflected the comments of many of the younger group. "I know what I want success to mean, but I am not there yet. I work in wellness so I know I want a healthy balance in everything. It is not just about your career. You need to have a family and home life that meets your needs in other ways and provides other challenges. I don't meet my personal checklist yet. I find myself staying late at work. I need to get my priorities straight in my life."

Beth said, "The ultimate success is to be happy. I think I am very successful. I have a loving husband, great parents, healthy children, and a job I enjoy."

Deborah, who is married and the mother of two, said, "I define success as feeling content. For me it is doing work that feels meaningful and rewarding. My job has an impact on individuals and it is rewarding. I am doing a pretty good job on the kid part. I am not doing such a good job on the husband part. It is all about work/kids/spouse/friends and me. I need to work on the spouse and friends. I need to figure out how to read a book or go to the gym. The balancing act is hard, but I feel pretty good today."

Deborah summed up the challenges faced by all working mothers. Having seen her own mother succeed and having her mother continue as a mentor makes balancing it all and achieving her goals easier.

Any mother would be proud of these grown children. They are thoughtful in their personal and professional lives. Working mothers can cut themselves some slack and be assured their children are just fine, will turn out well, and live happy, successful lives.

Chapter 14

My Mother Taught Me
She Is Proud of Me

We have heard from the grown children what success meant to them. How did the mothers feel about how their children turned out? The working mothers who were interviewed shared their perspectives.

Money Does Matter

The grown children interviewed and surveyed did not put money on the top of their lists when talking about success, but it was in the top four items listed. Money—or more accurately the financial independence it brings—was mentioned often by the mothers interviewed. Why?

We are all a product of our own experiences, and the mothers interviewed—the Baby Boomers, as we have been labeled—were raised by parents who had been profoundly impacted by the Depression. Almost every household of my parents' generation, called the Silent Generation, suffered a financial loss. I heard stories throughout my childhood about my paternal grandfather losing his business and my grandparents' house being repossessed by the bank. Even years after these events, my father had to drop out of college for a year and work in a factory to earn money for the tuition so he could return to school.

The Silent Generation saved and saved and saved. Most of these parents did not even consider giving their children cars or help with the down payment on a house. They had seen rough times, and they were afraid they might need the money later in life.

The mothers interviewed, the Baby Boomers, grew up in a time of relative economic prosperity, as did their children. Two working parents further increased the disposable income for many families interviewed. Rebelling against the frugal nature of our parents, many of us Baby Boomers gave our children everything. While we tried to teach our children about money, it is hard to teach value when there is no scarcity. As one mother said, "We spoiled our kids big time."

Thus, financial independence was on many mothers' list of success factors. The mothers knew from experience that a certain level of income was required. They may also have realized, a little late, that their own parents had a point—saving money has advantages.

Every mother knows her children must grow up and leave the nest, and that means being able to take care of themselves, especially financially. When Sylvia described why her children were successful, she said, "They are relatively secure financially. Importantly, they are off 'the family payroll.'" Janet believes her son Kevin learned good lessons about money. "Because money was very tight in our household, he is very conscientious in taking care of his family's finances."

Some mothers, however, were very explicit that money was not the top of the success checklist. Myra said, "Money is not very important except as a tool to enable you." Susan G said she and her husband did not feel that having lots of money was evidence of success. However, when she explained why she considered her children successful, her list included "financially independent" and "frugal."

Personally, I always thought money was important. As a single parent for over a decade, I knew the anxiety of waking in the middle of the night wondering if I would be able support two children on my own. I made sure my children knew bills had to be paid and insisted they get summer jobs from the time they were sixteen.

To answer the question, "Will my child get a job?" the survey indicated yes, and the mother's status of being a career or stay-at-home mother was not the determining factor. Survey results indicate that a majority of grown children of both working and stay-at-home mothers were employed. Since education impacts employment opportunities, the chart below shows employment by the education level of the mother. The chart below shows the answers to the question, "What are you doing today? If more than one answer applies to you, please select what you spend the majority of your time doing." The choices are described below.

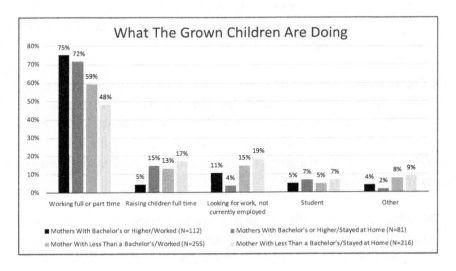

There were very similar results for the children of highly educated mothers. The only difference is that, regardless of the education level of the mother, more children whose mothers stayed at home were also raising children full time, perhaps because they had seen their mothers do this.

Somewhere in there is a balance. Joanne spoke for many mothers when she said, "It is not about money, but to be happy, my daughters need to be able to support their lifestyle."

Ultimately, seeing children able to support themselves financially and choose their own level of lifestyle was a success indicator for the mothers.

Life Skills Are a Sign of Success

Mothers described their children's success using terms very different than those used by their children. Mothers knew that skills like "independence" and "resiliency" were not a given; they considered achievement of these a success. Susan G considers both of her children to be extremely successful since "they are balanced, resilient, good-natured, and have a keen sense of humor."

Lisa B says, "I consider my children to be very successful. They are making the right decisions at the right times and with the right amount of parental involvement. They have moved from 'tell us what to do' to 'give us your advice.' They have an increasing amount of resiliency and can rebound from disappointments."

Marcia says, "My children are totally successful. They are independent and comfortable in their own skin. They are balanced. They can take a knock and it will not change the way they think about themselves. Neither one walks away from challenges. They don't wait to be asked, they move forward. If they feel strongly about something, they have no problem telling you what they think. They are comfortable with who they are."

Gay says, "They are confident. They feel good about where they are. They know what is important and they prioritize. They think they have something to contribute. They take care of themselves. They work hard on whatever it is they are doing."

Mothers knew that to be successful in life, even characteristics that children assume are obvious are hard won. They were proud their children had acquired these life skills.

Passions Should Be Followed

The mothers agreed with their children that passion, however defined, is critical to happiness and success. Mothers did not just talk about their children's careers but their other passions in life as well.

Kathleen says, "I define success as being passionate about what you do every day in your personal and professional life. My daughter Alix has this passion, and it is why she is in human services."

Karen said, "To me, the key measure of success is to care about people other than yourself. I was very fortunate to get a scholarship to college. It had a huge impact on me, and my children knew this." Her daughter Beth has been influenced by her mother's background. "My mother had to rely on scholarships to go to school. She taught her kids that giving back is important. I am passionate about being able to give back. I am a huge advocate for education, another thing she taught me, so I combine both and contribute to financial aid. That way others will have the opportunity for a good education.

No one can take away your education." This is a passion passed from mother to daughter and one they can share.

Mothers Agree Family and Friends Are Important

Mothers were pleased that their children valued family and friends. Lisa C says, "The boys are both empathetic and caring, which is the best definition of success."

Joanie says, "I consider my daughters incredibly successful. They are happy and well adjusted. They are all in good solid relationships. I never measured success by the schools they attended or the money they were making. All of them have tremendous friends. In many ways they are more successful than I am."

Judy says, "I define success as being stable within herself. Knowing who she is. Having good partners. My daughters are both great mothers, daughters, wives, and sisters. They are incredible."

When asked about whether her children were successful, Myra said, "Yes. All of them. They have their physical and mental health. They have work they love. They have families they love. They know it is all about people and how you care for them."

Polly feels strongly that her children are successful. She says they are mature, articulate, caring, have a great group of friends, are fun to be around, and love their mother. It's nice to know that all the love mothers provide their children is reciprocated.

Susan M says, "I love my daughters and how they turned out. I know in the second half of my life I will be well taken care of."

Elaine, mother of three, said, "On the personal happiness side, they believe they are successful and have friends and do many things. By my definition they are not yet completely successful because I define success as married with children." Okay, it's still true that many mothers want grandchildren.

As Long as You're Happy

The working mothers had a broader definition of "success" than their children gave them credit for. Family, friends, and passion topped the list—as long as there was enough money for the children to pay the bills on their own.

I wish the same for my own children. My daughter Sarah lives outside New York and has always worked in financial services. She is married and the mother of three young children. My son Paul lives on the West Coast, is married, and works at a technology company. Their lives are very different. Sarah spends her weekends chauffeuring her children to their various activities and doing art projects. At this point in Paul's life, he has time after work and on weekends to go to the gym and try new restaurants. Still, at the core, they are alike. We can get together as a family after months of being apart, and within minutes everyone is laughing and catching up on what we missed between phone calls and Facebook.

If asked whether my children are successful, my answer is yes, and I would use many of the same terms as the mothers interviewed. My children are financially independent, have loving families and good friends, and enjoy the work they are doing. Are they always happy? No. Life is complicated and presents them with challenges on a regular basis, as is the case for most people. But they meet problems head on and keep going. What makes them successful is they are able to enjoy where they are now in their lives and take pleasure in planning for the future.

I was on a difficult hike once when the group leader told me that the secret to climbing a steep incline was to just put one foot in front of the other and keep going. That is what I and many other working mothers have taught our children. Even when we are not certain if we are going in the right direction, we move forward and enjoy the journey.

The working mothers of the Baby Boomer generation have come full circle. First we surprised our parents by choosing to work full time. Now we have surprised our children by appreciating that each generation will have its own path to happiness. We are fine if our children's paths diverge from ours.

Working mothers raised independent children and were supportive of their children's choices. Like every parent, they just want their children to be happy. As Karen says, "I define success for my children however they want to define it."

It is up to each working mother to define what success means to her and what it means for her children when they are grown. The mothers interviewed did not regret working, and their children did not express regret about being raised by a working mother.

I hope the stories from these families and the numbers from the survey will give working mothers the confidence that their children will be fine. As we have seen, the grown children are happy, successful adults.

Working mothers need to share their experiences with each other. Reach out to other women for advice and support and provide it in return. Listen now to the words of advice of the working mothers and their children.

Chapter 15

Advice from Working Mothers and Their Children

Working mothers and their grown children interviewed had plenty of advice for the working mothers of today. Mothers covered a few more topics, not unusual given their longer history of child rearing, and those thoughts are at the end. The quotes are actual quotes from the mothers and children interviewed. They are not attributed since so many individuals had the same concepts.

1. **Stay Involved: Your Children Want You as Part of Their Lives**

   From the children's perspective:

   "Be involved and know what is going on."

   "Go to your child's sporting events and music performances. Show support for your child."

   "Take advantage of the weekends with your children."

   "Make the effort. Even if you can't be there, call. Let them know you are thinking of them."

   "Parents should be as active in their children's lives as possible. The kids need to understand you will be there for them, not to baby them, but to have their back."

From the mothers' perspective:

"Try to spend as much time with your children as possible. Don't waste your weekends cleaning your house. Take a day off from work if your child has a play."

"Vote with your feet. Be there, be around as much as you can."

"Keep an open dialogue with your kids."

"Love your child to death, let them know they are deeply loved and always have a safe place and you will always show up for them."

2. Don't Feel Guilty: You Are a Role Model for Your Children

From the children's perspective:

"It was great for me to have a mom who worked and was happy. I certainly got enough attention and support as a kid."

"Mothers need to believe in themselves and their choices. It is easy to doubt, so trust your gut."

"I never felt my mom was all about work, she was my mom. Seeing the choices she made, I feel like it inspired me. Advice? Do what my mom did."

"I would definitely encourage moms to stay in the workplace. It was an inspiration to me that my mother worked and was successful. I have huge respect for her. Moms are inspiring their kids to be successful."

From the mothers' perspective:

_____

"The kids respect you when you are happy.
They are happy when you are happy."

"Let go of the guilt. The guilt will kill you. Enjoy life."

"If a problem occurs, it would probably
have occurred if you worked or not."

"You are giving your kids a great role
model by keeping it all together."

"Stick with it—it's a short stretch. It's maybe twelve years
they need you and you'll work forty to fifty years. It's a
sacrifice in some ways but a gift in other ways to your kids."

"As a working mother, your children need to
see you valuing yourself and your efforts."

3. **Be the Parent: Help Them Grow Up to Be Responsible
    Adults**

From the children's perspective:

_____

"Kids need structure. Don't be afraid to be strict."

"You don't need to be buddies with your kid. You
want to care about them, but as a mother. There
is a balance somewhere in the middle."

"Treat your kids like adults and have
honest conversations with them."

"Teach them to be decent people."

From the mothers' perspective:

"Don't make the mistake of being friends with
your kids. Parents must set expectations."

"Kids need boundaries and certainty in their lives
even though they don't always appreciate it."

"Teach children it takes hard work to get ahead."

"Teach them to care about people. Be kind to others."

"Your children will grow up to be responsible adults as
long as you are lovingly consistent and trust your instincts."

4. Build Resilience: Teach Them How to Solve Problems

From the children's perspective:

"Don't be afraid to let your kid fail every
now and again. It is good for them."

"Give the kids room to make mistakes."

"Let them have experiences."

From the mothers' perspective:

"There are very few fatal mistakes you can make. As long
as you protect their safety and health, they will be okay."

"Kids are more resilient than you think. They get
knocked down and they come up again. We think
they are like papier-mâché, they get a ding and
they are never the same, but that's not true."

"Tell your child failing is okay and they need to
pick themselves up, learn from it, and move on."

"Adversity is a good thing. Let your children fail."

"Teach them how to solve problems.
Don't just give them the solution."

5. Be Flexible: Each Child Is Different

From the children's perspective:

"Kids are different. Not every kid is going to
be what the parents expect them to be."

"There isn't a handbook on how to raise your kids.
Kids are different from you with different problems
and needs, so you need to be adaptable."

"Respect children's differences. If they show
interest in something, help them pursue it but don't
force things on your kids. Don't force children to
become something they do not want to be."

From the mothers' perspective:

"Don't just assume if you give them enough information
your kids will be exactly the way you want them."

"Try to think of your kids as people and not just your kids."

"Make every child feel special, because she is."

6. Share the Responsibility: Let Others Take a Role in Raising the Children

From the children's perspective:

"Parents should 'split the voice.' What are you
each good at? My dad is good to talk to about
some things and my mom about others."

"It's not all on you. If you have a two-parent household, work should be shared. If you are a single parent, get the best childcare you can."

"Always talk with older mothers. Seek out their advice and ask them to share their knowledge and experience."

From the mothers' perspective:

"Before you have kids you should have a clear understanding of the shared role of parenting with your spouse. There are a lot of logistics, and sharing makes a difference. Have honest, open negotiations and reach a clear understanding of how parenting will work in your family."

"Good childcare can make or break your ability to be a working parent. Once you take it off the table as a concern, it makes a huge difference."

"If you do not have a family support system, create it yourself."

"Let go of the notion there is only one right way to do things. Other people have good ideas too."

"When you are navigating work as a mother, you need to find someone who's been there, done that."

7. Don't Bring Work Home: When Home, Focus on the Family

From the children's perspective:

"As a working mom, don't bring stress from work back home."

"Work is stressful, but put it away."

"My mom did it right. When she was home, she
was home, and she totally separated things."

From the mothers' perspective:

"Kids don't understand double-tasking. My son once said,
'It doesn't count that you're here if you're still working.'"

"Leave work at work. Go home and have some fun."

"If you are working from home, have set hours
so the kids know when you are 'off.'"

"Put the kids to bed first and work later."

8. Look at the Big Picture: Don't Sweat the Small Stuff

From the mothers' perspective:

"Don't sweat the small stuff, and
most of it is the small stuff."

"Stop and think before you react. Put it in perspective."

"Don't take it all so seriously. Relax and enjoy yourself."

"Learn what you care about. Find the things that matter
to you and do them fully. Don't worry about the rest."

"Be patient. Your child will get through
it, and you will get through it."

9. Times Flies: Enjoy Your Children and Have Fun

From the mothers' perspective:

"The days crawl, the years fly. Sometimes
you think you will always be changing
diapers, but of course you won't be."

"Be joyful along the way."

"Take every opportunity to be in the moment
and play and laugh—they grow up so fast."

"Slow down a little and spend some quiet time.
Soon you'll be asking yourself, 'Where did
the eighteen years go for each child?'"

10. Final Thoughts from Working Mothers

"Being a working mother is the hardest thing you'll
ever do, but I wouldn't trade it for anything,"

"I knew intellectually, but did not fully appreciate,
that being a mother is a lifelong commitment.
You never really get through worrying about
them. Now, of course, they worry about me."

"I think of us working mothers as raising children who can
be as proud of their mothers as they are of their fathers."

"I can't imagine my life without children. Being
a mother is more of who I am than an executive.
I never, ever regret having my children."

Thank you again to all of the working mothers and their
children who contributed to this project.

Endnotes

1   "An Assessment of Paid Time Off in the U.S.: Implications for employees, companies and the economy." *Oxford Economics*, Feb. 2014.

2   "Breadwinner Moms, Mothers are the Sole or Primary Provider in Four in Ten Households with Children: Public Conflicted about the Growing Trend." Pew Research, Social and Demographic Trends, May 29, 2013. www.pewsocialtrends.org

3   Consortium on Chicago Schools Research. "Free to Fail or On-Track to College: Why Grades Drop When Students Enter High School and What Adults Can Do About It." Research Brief April 2014. The University of Chicago Consortium on Chicago Schools Research.

4   Galinsky, Ellen. *Ask The Children: What America's Children Really Think about Working Parents*. William Morrow and Company, Inc., 1999.

5   "Live Births, Deaths, Marriages, and Divorces: 1960 to 2007." Table 78. U.S. Census Bureau, Statistical Abstract of the United States: 2011.

6   Milkie, Melissa A. and Kei M. Nomaguchi and Kathleen E. Denny. "Does the Amount of Time Mothers Spent with Children or Adolescents Matter?" *Journal of Marriage and Family*, April 2015.

7   "New AARP Survey Finds Grandparents Play Essential Role." March 29, 2012. www.aarp.org/abput-aarp/press-center

8   West, Martin R. and Guido Schwerdt. "The Middle School Plunge: Achievement tumbles when young students change schools." *Education Next*, Spring 2012/Vol. 12, No. 2.

9   Youth Risk Behavior Surveillance Bullying Statistics—United States 2013. Morbidity and Mortality Weekly Report, June 13, 2014. Centers for Disease Control. www.pacer.org.

Appendix 1: Discussion Guides

Topics for Self Reflection

Many of the mothers interviewed said they wish they had been more thoughtful about having children and the impact it would have on their careers and their marriages. They were glad they had their children and kept working, but felt they could have been more prepared. Below are some questions for women to consider when they are making decisions on managing work and family.

1. What do I like about my job?
2. What are my career goals?
3. What are my personal goals?
4. What personal sacrifices am I willing to make to achieve my career goals?
5. What career sacrifices am I willing to make to achieve my personal goals?
6. What are the things most important to *my children* and how do I find the time to do them?
7. What are the things *I* most want to do with my children and how do I find the time to do them?
8. What part of my home/family life am I willing to delegate to others?
9. What do I expect my spouse to do as part of our home/family life?
10. What trade-offs are my spouse and I willing to make in order to ensure:
    a. We find time as a couple?
    b. I have personal time?
    c. My spouse has personal time?

Topics for Grown Children and Mothers

All of the mothers and grown children interviewed expressed interest in the topic of work and family. While the children interviewed had all grown up with a working mother, few of the families had ever discussed the topic. Below are some questions for mothers and their grown children to start a dialogue. While there is no changing history, the discussion might help the grown children as they nurture their own families.

Mothers Ask Their Children

1. What are your favorite memories of your childhood?
2. What did we do together that you want to replicate with your family?
3. What new experiences do you want to have with your family?
4. How did you see the parenting role of your parent(s) when you were growing up?
5. What do you think we each taught you to be successful in life?
6. What were some of the lessons you learned from other adults in your life (e.g. teachers, grandparents, coaches, etc.).
7. What did we all forget to teach you that you had to learn on your own?
8. How do you define success for yourself and where are you on your own checklist?
9. How did you feel about my working and did your feelings change over time?
10. Now that you are an adult, what advice would you give working mothers about raising their children?

Children Ask Their Mothers

1. What are your favorite memories of my childhood?
2. What part of raising children did you find difficult?
3. Looking back, are there things you would have done differently?
4. When you were raising me, there were not as many working mothers in the workplace as there are today. How did you figure it all out?
5. How did having children impact your career?
6. Parenting:
   a. If raised in two-parent home: How did you as parents divide up the parenting roles?
   b. If raised in single parent home: How did you manage as a single parent?
7. What did you try to teach me to be successful in life?
8. Looking back, is there anything you forgot to teach me?
9. What do you wish you knew then that you know now?
10. What wisdom would you pass onto young mothers raising children today?

Lessons for Mothers to Share

Working mothers, or women who plan to become mothers, need to reach out to others with experience to see what they have learned. There are many common issues, and it makes sense to get ideas from people who have been successful at raising children while working. If you are uncomfortable talking to women in your own organization, use your network or those of your friends to find working mothers. If you are a working mother yourself, make time to share your experiences with others. Start the discussion from the topics below, depending on where you are in your life and what you want to do.

Pregnancy:

1. Is there a right time from a career perspective to have children?
2. How did you handle pregnancy and working?

Maternity Leave:

1. How did you tell your boss you were pregnant?
2. What arrangements were made to handle your work while you were out?
3. How much maternity leave did you take and was it enough?

Return to Work:

1. When you came back to work, how did you feel?
2. Did people treat you differently?
3. How did you gear back into the workplace?

Career Planning:

1. How can I be sure I am still on the fast track even though I have had a baby?
2. If I want to stay working at my current level but do not want to take on any extra work right after having a baby, how can I communicate this?
3. If I want to stay working but cut my hours, what is the best way to do that?

Role of the Spouse:

1. How do you and your spouse divide up the parenting duties?
2. What works well and what doesn't?

Child Rearing:

1. What are the toughest parts of being a parent in: preschool, elementary school, middle school, and high school?
2. What are the best things to do with children:
     a. Daily?
     b. On weekends?
     c. At holiday times?
     d. For vacation?
3. What is the one piece of advice you want to give me?

Appendix 2: Biographies of the Families Interviewed

Prior to the Survey Monkey project, twenty-seven middle class families were interviewed. These interviews provided the questions for the survey and resulted in sixty-eight in-depth discussions with working mothers and their now adult children who had been raised with a full-time working mother. Their stories reinforce the data provided by the survey. Or perhaps it is the data that reinforces their stories.

The mothers interviewed had careers in accounting, advertising, banking, broadcasting, consulting, education, farming, health care, legal, manufacturing, non-profit, oil and gas, technology and venture capital industries. These women became successful in their chosen careers, but they started at the bottom just like everyone else. Approximately 60 percent of the couples remained married and 40 percent were divorced, compared to the 50 percent national divorce rate previously quoted. Not all of their children were interviewed due to work schedules or lack of interest.

Meet the families who agreed to be interviewed for this book. The mothers are listed first with their background, and then their children's names and backgrounds.

Elaine has a BS from Boston University, MS from Columbia University in community psychiatry, and PhD from New York University in industrial and organizational psychology, which she received while working and having one child. She is dean of executive education at a major college, and her career spans roles as a business leader and general manager, human resources executive, private and public board member, and organizational consultant. Jessica has a BA from Bennington College in environmental science, architecture, and politics and a master's in urban and regional planning from the University of Michigan. Jessica is married and working as a sustainability specialist in an engineering design firm in Boston. Peter E has a BA in journalism and advertising from the University of Wisconsin and received his MBA at Babson while continuing to work full time, most recently as vice president of growth and partnerships in a start-up in San Francisco. Matt has a BA in communications from the University of Wisconsin. He has worked as a talent manager in the film industry and is currently the New York steward of the brand of a craft rye distillery.

Gay has a bachelor in fine arts from the University of Texas and is the founder and CEO of her own advertising agency, T3. Gay founded her agency with a cashed-in IRA, two employees, and a typewriter. Today it is the largest woman-owned, independent agency in the United States with Fortune 500 clients and a revolutionary daycare system called T3 and Under. Gay divorced her first husband when her daughter was three and remarried when her daughter was young, gaining two stepsons. The children were raised in Texas. Rebecca has a BA in marketing from the Laboratory Institute of Merchandising, worked in the fashion industry in New York, and founded a clothing and accessories company in Austin. Ben has a BA from Texas A&M, is married with one child, and works as the chief innovation officer at the family advertising company. Sam has a BA from the University of Texas and recently sold the Austin-based company he co-founded and led as chief innovation officer.

Gina was a history major at Indiana University at Bloomington. Most of her career was on the real estate side of banking, and she is now a managing director of a consulting firm that focuses on profit improvement. Gina, who lives in Rhode Island, was divorced when her son was a teenager. Angus decided to forgo college to work in Silicon Valley, founding one firm he sold to a major technology company. He is now CEO of another technology company, which he elected to start in his home state of Rhode Island. He is married with two sons.

Janet claims she is retired but is writing and is a consultant and coach. With a BFA from Drake University, Janet started her career in New York City in executive search and then moved into human resources in the banking industry. She divorced when her son Kevin was five, raised him in New York, and did not remarry until Kevin was in high school. Kevin received his BA in sociology with a minor in criminology from the University of Colorado at Boulder. After a few start-ups, Kevin moved into the advertising industry in New York where he is now a senior executive at a major firm, focusing on the technology industry. Kevin is married and has two daughters.

Joanie has a BA in economics from Bates College, MBA from the Wharton School at the University of Pennsylvania, and a master's in accounting from Bentley University. She spent her entire career in the finance departments of technology companies, with thirty years as a chief financial officer. She and her husband raised their daughters in the suburbs of Boston. Lindsay has a BA in sociology and Spanish from Gettysburg College and a master's in media and communications from Brunel University in the UK. She is married and working as an account supervisor at a public relations firm in Boston. Caitlyn has a BA in psychology from Hamilton College. She worked for several years as a mental health research assistant at hospitals in Boston and is now getting her PhD at the California School of Professional Psychology in San Francisco. Susannah has a BA in art history, English and classical studies from Brandeis University and has worked in customer relations and business development in several technology companies in the Boston and New York areas.

Joanne has a BA in animal science from the University of Rhode Island and MBA in accounting from the University of Connecticut, a degree she received while working and being the mother of a young child. Joanne worked as a bank teller, an accountant, in research administration, and finally moved into the planning and budgeting side of higher education where she has held senior positions at two large state universities. She and her husband raised their daughters on a farm in Connecticut. Megan has a BS in management and accounting from Tulane University and a master's in sustainability and environmental management from the Harvard University Extension School. Megan started her career as a financial analyst at a university and then moved into sustainability manager positions at two universities. She now lives in Washington, DC. Catherine has a BA in human development and family studies from the University of Connecticut, worked in administration at a university, and now is a case manager in a guardianship program for incapacitated adults in the Boston area.

Judy has a MA in communications from Emerson College and an MBA in health care administration from Golden Gate University. Her first career was as a clinical speech pathologist. Later she moved into compensation consulting for a large global consulting firm. She and her husband relocated from Chicago to San Francisco where they raised their two girls. Jennifer has a BA in psychology and MBA from Cornell University. She is married with two children. After various careers in education and technology, she is now president and COO of a global B Corp for-profit company. Deborah has a BA in American studies from Cornell University and an MBA from Harvard Business School. She is married with two daughters. After an early career in advertising in New York and London, she is living back in the San Francisco area and is in executive search in consumer technology and marketing.

Karen has a BS in mathematics from Trinity College in Hartford, and an MBA from the Wharton School of the University of Pennsylvania. Karen started her career as a securities analyst on Wall Street, but quickly moved to the corporate side where she worked for several technology companies, becoming controller of a major publicly traded technology company. Karen is now bringing her experience to corporate and non-profit boards. She has been married since she was twenty-four years old. Beth has a BA in economics and Spanish from Trinity College and an MBA in marketing from Boston College. She is married, has two children, and works in marketing and communications for a major insurance company in the Boston area. David attended Syracuse University and is a photographer in Hawaii.

Kathleen has a BA from Merrick College and is head of human resources at a large human services company. She was divorced when her daughter was two years old and her stay-at-home ex-husband got residential custody of the child through high school. Kathleen remarried when her daughter was eight and gained a stepson and stepdaughter. Alix has a BA from UMass Lowell in psychology and philosophy and worked as a program supervisor in a girl's residential home. Alix is now studying at the University of Pennsylvania for dual degrees—an MSEd in counseling and mental health services and an MS Philosophy ED in professional counseling.

Kristine has a BS in physics from Yale, her MS in electrical engineering from Northeastern University, and an MBA from Harvard Business School. Kristine started her career as an engineer in a high-tech company, went into consulting, returned to technology where she rose to be CEO of a publicly traded company, and is now in executive search. She was divorced when her children were young and she raised them in the suburbs of Boston. Jamie has a BA in finance and economics from Indiana University at Bloomington and is a financial analyst at a major technology company in the Midwest. Rory has a BA in accounting and finance from Indiana University at Bloomington and is a CPA at a major accounting firm in Boston.

Laura H has a BA in political science and French literature from Wellesley College and a JD from Harvard Law School, where she met her husband who was attending the business school. Laura is a partner at the Boston law firm she joined out of law school and she and her husband raised their sons in the suburbs of Boston. Zach has a BA from Middlebury in economics and Chinese and worked in financial services out of college in New York and Hong Kong before starting a company with his brother. He now works for a technology start-up in Northern California. Nick has a BA from Davidson College in history. After college he joined his brother in the start-up and is now a whiskey and scotch specialist in the Boston area.

Lisa B is executive vice president of human resources for a major health care company. She has a BA in modern languages from Trinity College and MBA from the University of Connecticut. Married for over thirty years, she and her husband raised their children in Massachusetts. Their son Daniel N graduated with a BA in history and Spanish from Bates and is working as a program manager at a research firm in Boston. Daughter Laura N has a BA in English from Skidmore and works as a research associate at the same firm as her brother, but in the New York office.

Lisa C, now retired, had a career in management in the broadcasting industry. With her BA in ancient studies from Barnard and an MBA from Harvard Business School, Lisa and her husband raised their sons in New York, Chicago, and Providence as the family moved around for Lisa's job. Drew has a BA in economics from Occidental College, works for a wealth management firm, and is renovating multi-family homes. Gray attended Johnson and Wales University and Community College of Rhode Island and is the manager of a restaurant.

Marcia has BS from Brown University in chemistry and mathematics, an MA in chemistry from Columbia, and an MBA from Harvard Business School. She started her career at a technology company, spent most of her career in venture capital, and is now working with early stage technology companies. She and her husband raised their children in the suburbs of Boston. Phil has a BA from Brown University in East Asian history and now works in the corporate development group of a growing technology company in the Boston area. Anne has a BA in economics from Brown University, a master's from the London School of Economics, and is working at an Internet technology company in New York.

Maryalice has a BA degree in economics from Rutgers University. Out of college she joined a large technology company in sales and progressed to sales management and then consulting jobs. She became a partner in a large technology consulting firm, a managing director of a large professional services company, and is currently an associate director at a major accounting firm focused on strategy

173

work for life science clients. She and her husband raised their daughters in a small town in Pennsylvania and got divorced when her youngest was in college. Sarah D has a BA in history from Middlebury College and is a management consultant in Boston. Caroline D has a BA in economics and American studies from Middlebury College and is in financial services in New York.

Myra has a BA in government from Cornell University and an MBA and a DBA in entrepreneurship from Harvard Business School. Myra's first career was in commercial real estate. She then got her MBA when she had three children. After business school she went into marketing and then co-founded a large retailer which she left to get her PhD and go into teaching and research. Myra and her husband divorced when her youngest was in middle school, and she did not remarry until the children were grown. The children grew up in Illinois, Michigan, and Massachusetts. Holly has a BS from Cornell University in civil engineering and an MBA from Harvard Business School and is married with two daughters. After a career in engineering and construction and then low-cost housing, she is now a full time volunteer. Jean has a BA from Cornell University in psychology, an MA in education from UMass, and a Doctor of Veterinary Medicine degree from Virginia Tech, is widowed, and has her own mobile veterinary practice in Florida. Rick has a BA from Dominican University and an MBA from a joint program run by the University of California at Berkeley and Columbia. He is a product manager for a large communications company in northern California, divorced, and the father of two children.

Nancy has a BA in history from San Jose State and a second BA in sociology from UC Santa Barbara. She is working in the wine industry as a consultant helping launch new brands. Nancy was widowed very young and remarried several years later. Nancy and her husband raised their daughter Nicole A while building their own vineyard in Northern California and the couple divorced when Nicole was in graduate school. Nicole has a BS in biology from Lewis and Clark College and an MS in molecular plant systematics from Florida International University. She lives in Barcelona with her husband and two children, works for an American wine importer, and has her own travel business.

Pattie has a BA in marketing from the University of Memphis and an MS in human resource development from Villanova University, which she earned while working full time. Pattie has had a career in human resources in the technology industry, holding the top position in both a large public firm and a start-up. She and her husband raised their son in Arizona, Massachusetts, and Colorado. Chris has a BA in history from Stonehill College, spent two years in AmeriCorps out of college and is now working as a veterinary technician in Colorado while taking courses to become a certified dog trainer.

Polly, now retired, has a BA from Brown University and an MBA from Harvard Business School. She has worked at four different banks in senior credit positions in New York City. She raised her children in the suburbs. Polly and her husband divorced and she did not remarry until her children were older. Mary graduated from Brown University with a BA, is married, and works for a bank in Ohio. Livey graduated from Johns Hopkins and is a lieutenant junior grade in the United States Navy.

Susan C has, for over thirty years, had her own consulting business focused on leadership development. She and her husband divorced when son Justin was ten. Justin was raised in Rhode Island and attended community college before starting his first career training horses. He is now building his career at a large defense contractor in Rhode Island.

Susan D has worked at five banks as a lending officer, moving from New York to Pittsburgh and now Atlanta. Susan has a BA from Wheaton College and an MBA from the Wharton School of the University of Pennsylvania. Peter D has a BA in religious studies and politics from Lafayette College, and an MA in religion from the University of Virginia. He lives with his wife in Boynton Beach, Florida, where he is content director at a research company. Maggie has a BS in fashion from Cornell and works in the fashion industry in New York. Katherine graduated from the University of Washington in St. Louis with a degree in marketing and Chinese and works in marketing for an airline in Atlanta.

Susan G has a BA in urban studies from Washington University in St. Louis and a master's in education from the Harvard University Graduate School of Education. Now a freelance writer and editor, Susan has spent her career working in communications in non-profit, education, and corporate environments. She and her husband raised their children outside of Boston. Danielle has a BA in English literature and Spanish from Washington University in St. Louis and works in a charter school in New York. Joshua has a BA in environmental science and Spanish from Middlebury and co-founded a food business in Harlem.

Susan F has a BA in economics from Brown University and her MBA from Boston University, a degree she pursued while working full time. She has spent her career in the oil and gas industry and is now at a consulting firm in Washington, DC. Susan and her husband raised their daughters in New Orleans, London, and Houston, divorcing when the youngest was a senior in high school. Elena has a BA in business from Tulane and a master's in public health from Emory, is married, and works for the US government in health care in Atlanta. Eva has a BA from Barry University, is the mother of a son, and works at a bank in Houston.

Susan M studied at UMass and holds a master's in management from Cambridge College, Cambridge, Massachusetts, a degree she received while working full time and raising two children with her husband. She spent her for-profit career in the financial services industry and is now chief operating and financial officer of a not-for-profit in New York. Susan and her husband raised their daughters in the suburbs of Boston and divorced when the youngest was a sophomore in high school. Nicole L has a BA in political science and statistics from Columbia University and an MA in statistics from the University of California, Santa Barbara. She works as a research education analyst for a firm in Washington, DC. Monique, who is married, has a BA in hospitality administration and management from Johnson & Wales University and now has a management position at a hotel chain in the Boston area.

Sylvia has a BA from Cornell University and a JD from Yale Law School. She practiced law briefly, worked for the State of Connecticut, then moved to a private investment firm. She is now is CEO of a non-profit. She and her husband raised their children in Connecticut and Massachusetts. Lauren J has a degree in music business management from Berklee College of Music, worked on the business side of the music industry, and is now in human resources for a non-profit. Evan has a BA in management from Roger Williams and is a manager at a restaurant.

Toni has a BA in government from Smith College and a JD from the University of Pennsylvania Law School, which she earned while married and raising two small boys. After getting divorced, Toni moved to Boston, spent her for-profit career in law in Boston, and remarried. Retired from the practice of law, she now works to get more women on corporate boards of directors and raises money for her alma mater, Smith. Jeffrey has a BA in political science from Washington University in St. Louis and an MS in business and financial services from Boston University. He is married with two children and has spent his career in financial services. He is now a senior vice president of a money manager in New York. David has a BA in history from Amherst College and a master's in education from Boston College. He has always been in education, as a teacher, coach, dean of students, and now as head of school of an independent school in the south. David is married with three children.

Vicki has a BA in chemistry from Duke University. She and her husband got married right out of college and moved around the country for both of their jobs, raising their children in St. Louis, San Diego, and Pittsburgh. Vicki's career has been in the manufacturing industry, first in technical sales, then management, and finally as CEO of two publicly traded companies. Lauren H has a BA from Penn State University in kinesiology and exercise science and is now a program manager in New Jersey for a company that provides wellness plans for major corporations. Matt is attending college.

Appendix 3: Demographic Data of the Survey Participants

Grown Children of Working Mothers

1. Number of participants: 374
2. Gender:

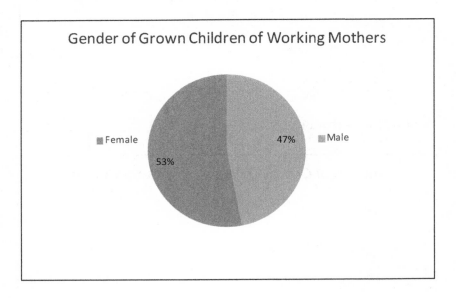

179

3. Age range:

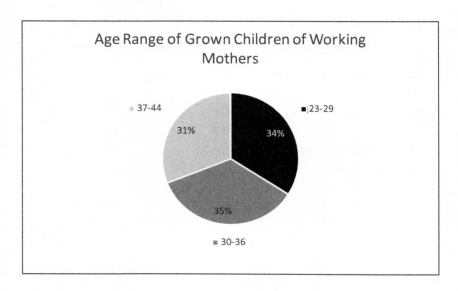

4. Race/ethnicity:

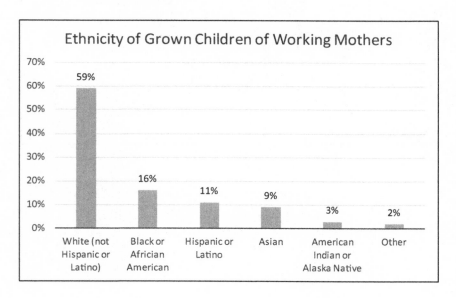

5. Who they primarily lived with through high school:

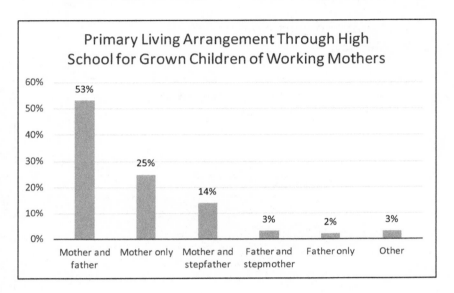

Primary Living Arrangement Through High School for Grown Children of Working Mothers

- Mother and father: 53%
- Mother only: 25%
- Mother and stepfather: 14%
- Father and stepmother: 3%
- Father only: 2%
- Other: 3%

6. Where they live now:

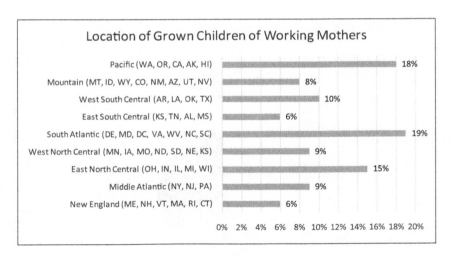

Location of Grown Children of Working Mothers

- Pacific (WA, OR, CA, AK, HI): 18%
- Mountain (MT, ID, WY, CO, NM, AZ, UT, NV): 8%
- West South Central (AR, LA, OK, TX): 10%
- East South Central (KS, TN, AL, MS): 6%
- South Atlantic (DE, MD, DC, VA, WV, NC, SC): 19%
- West North Central (MN, IA, MO, ND, SD, NE, KS): 9%
- East North Central (OH, IN, IL, MI, WI): 15%
- Middle Atlantic (NY, NJ, PA): 9%
- New England (ME, NH, VT, MA, RI, CT): 6%

Grown Children of Stay-at-Home Mothers

1. Number of participants: 307
2. Gender:

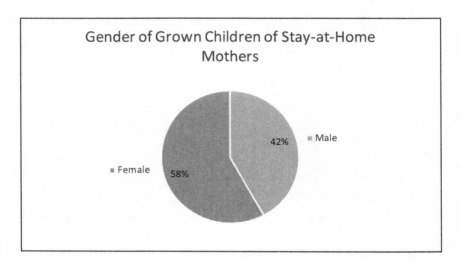

Gender of Grown Children of Stay-at-Home Mothers

42% Male

Female 58%

3. Age range:

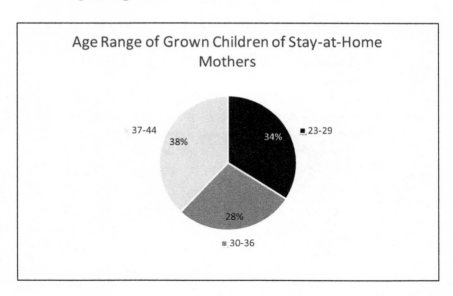

Age Range of Grown Children of Stay-at-Home Mothers

37-44
38%

34% 23-29

28%

30-36

4. Race/ethnicity:

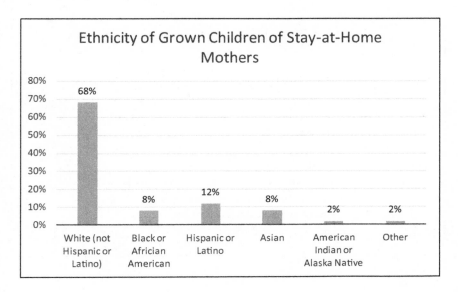

5. Who they primarily lived with through high school:

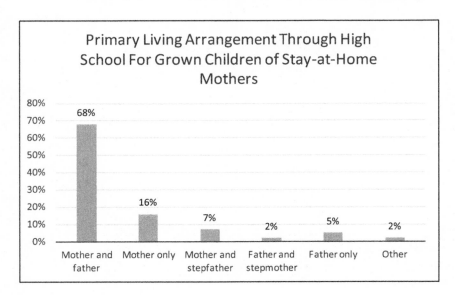

6. Where they live now:

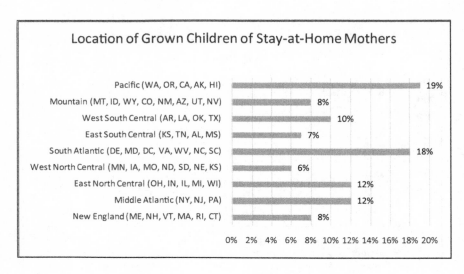

About the Author

Pamela F. Lenehan was a managing director in investment banking at Credit Suisse First Boston; an officer of Oak Industries, a NYSE listed company that was acquired by Corning; and CFO of a high-tech start-up. She is now on the boards of directors of three publicly traded companies, Monotype Imaging, Civitas Solutions, and American Superconductor. While raising her daughter and son, she was a single parent for eleven years and remarried when her children were in twelfth and eighth grades, creating a blended family that includes two step-daughters. She is now the proud grandmother of five.

For over thirty years, Lenehan has managed an informal women's network connecting corporate women in the Boston area for dinner and creating an "old girl" network. She is on the board of the Center for Women & Enterprise, which helps women start and grow businesses; co-chair of the Boston chapter of Women Corporate Directors; and a member of the Brown University Women's Leadership Council.

In her long career on Wall Street and in the corporate environment, it was expected that work and family lives would be kept separate, but Lenehan saw firsthand the family and career issues faced by women and men trying to be good parents while progressing in their careers. She wrote this book because she believes it is time for working mothers to step forward and talk about the challenges—and joys—of combining work and family. Lenehan is passionate about giving women (and men) of the next generation the confidence that their children will turn out well.

CPSIA information can be obtained at www.ICGtesting.com
Printed in the USA
BVOW08s0828030316

438914BV00001B/16/P